CW00546735

For ________________________,

The world truly yearns for individuals like you, who have the heart, passion, and potential to create meaningful impact.

Your unique gifts and vision are not just wanted—they are needed.

I wanted to share this book with you because I see in you the kind of entrepreneur the world genuinely needs.

May these pages inspire you as much as I believe in you.

To the journey ahead.

BET ON YOURSELF

BET ON YOURSELF

Your Testostrone-Free Guide to Being Your Own Boss

SARAH TURNER

Hardcover ISBN: 979-8-9900410-2-8
Paperback ISBN: 979-8-9900410-1-1
eBook ISBN: 979-8-9900410-0-4

CONTENTS

Bet Your Bottom Dollar **ix**

Chapter 1: (Don't) Bet like a Bro 1

Chapter 2: Don't Trade Your Old Boss for a Worse One 25

Chapter 3: Labels Limit Growth 53

Chapter 4: Microbets Win the Game 75

Chapter 5: You Call the Shots 96

Chapter 6: Your Relationship with Money 118

Chapter 7: Find Healing through Marketing 151

Chapter 8: Make Your Life Happen 175

Chapter 9: What Comes Next? 187

The World as I See It **215**

Acknowledgments **219**

About the Author **221**

BET YOUR BOTTOM DOLLAR

The only person you are destined to become
is the person you decide to be.
—Ralph Waldo Emerson

One of the most misleading concepts people try to sell both women and entrepreneurs is that one day you can reach some proverbial mountaintop: you solve all your problems; you get cured; you cross the finish line and get the gold medal. Just buy this story, this product, this bullshit—then all will be well. As long as you follow the lead exactly, you'll become a skinny, symmetrical, trend-setting millionaire overnight—life satisfaction guaranteed!

The most misleading idea of all? That there's only one right way to do it. Every successful person's story becomes THE path, forgetting that the foundation of every successful entrepreneur is tapping into and amplifying the powerful combination of their unique skills, strengths, and passions.

The benefit of having a variety of entrepreneurial paths to learn from is that it allows us to identify shortcuts, avoid heartache, and find what works for us (while leaving the rest).

We need more examples of modern entrepreneurship for two very important reasons. First, because far too many people still believe entrepreneurship isn't the safe bet. Second, because the loud and risky "bropreneurs" (who dominate the current conversation) are scaring off the empathetic, tender, and kind souls—the very people we need considering entrepreneurship so they can be out there solving problems in this world. It's similar to the idea that the best leaders are those who aren't seeking power—they want to make a real change, but they're often reluctant.

We, as a collective, benefit when people with good hearts and intentions bet on themselves because they're the ones who think differently. They are the ones who ultimately create massive waves of positive change.

When I was choosing the title for this book, I was reluctant to call it *Bet on Yourself*. For some reason, "Why not bet on yourself this time?" feels entirely different in conversation than it does strewn across the cover of a book. *Flowers added for softness, of course. And if I could blow a dandelion puff across the pages as you opened this book, I totally would.*

The thing is, there are parts of entrepreneurship that feel a little cheesy. And it's not because entrepreneurship itself is the problem, but because we've all interacted with an entrepreneur who is. So before we go any further, I'll just say it: there is no mountaintop or finish line. Believe me, I've looked.

I've fought with every mindset, every hang-up, every concept we're about to cover, **and I still do**. Frequently. Each new layer of growth as an entrepreneur—from the first gig I took (party planning, if you can believe it) to breaking eight figures—has triggered a new layer of personal growth. At this point, I've learned to expect the triggers and prioritize personal development as a business practice. Entrepreneurship means I'm no longer using leftover time and energy at the end of my workday. Investing in my personal well-being directly impacts my business, creating a reinforcing loop and a cascade of benefits. It's a beautiful, occasionally gut-wrenching, but mostly life-giving journey.

That's what I want to show you here—how to "bet on yourself" as a practice.

I want to help you figure out what lights *you* up and gives you more freedom. Why? Because the world needs more empathetic, kind souls like you in a place of power, free from survival mode, and fully thriving.

I don't expect you to follow in my footsteps, though I'm definitely going to share some of my journey with you. And I don't expect you to become one of my students either, though I definitely share some of their stories too. I can't assume what kind of business you want to build or what path you'll have to take to get there, so I'd love to just walk alongside you for a while.

I'll share a little bit about the mindset shifts and simple steps that have helped me, my friends, and my students develop a deeper sense of self-trust and the confidence to bet on our own abilities. Then I'll step back and cheer you on as you learn to bet on yours.

Let's start with a mini case study from two dear friends of mine.

The Drunk and the Millionaire

My two friends grew up in the same neighborhood in Maryland, went to the same high school, and graduated together. From the outside looking in, they were pretty evenly matched in potential. They were both personable and relatively smart. Although they both had a bit of a rebellious streak and a tendency to become restless, they were hardworking (when they were interested in the task at hand) and got decent grades without much effort. But after high school, they took very different paths.

The first often told me she wanted to look back at her life and think, *Damn, that was a wild ride.* She traveled often and filled her free time with adventure, making sure she never felt bored. But with excitement at the forefront of her mind, she forgot who she was. She began to let others' beliefs and priorities influence her decisions. Soon she didn't recognize herself. It was as if she woke up from a dream, looked around, and wondered, *How the F did I get here?*

On the day she married her partner in adventure, she told me she felt like she was caught on a runaway train where the only options were to jump out at neck-breaking speeds or to allow it to crash head-on. Either choice would cause tremendous damage and certain death. She said it would be easier to deal with an inevitable divorce than to face the judgments and pressure of the people around her.

To cope, she started drinking. Heavily. She drank to tap back into her rebellious side, to numb what she had become, and to hide from her growing sense of self-loathing. Eventually, she became impossible to recognize. The most frightening moment was when her self-loathing turned into suicidal thoughts. I was genuinely afraid for her life at times and grateful to see her go to rehab.

The second friend lived a much more calm, fulfilling, and prosperous life. She went on to build a wildly successful business that had a real impact on the world. She took a long, hard look at the areas of her life that were out of alignment and committed herself to finding solutions. First, she started a modest freelancing business, solving small problems in her own life and in the lives of her clients.

She soon realized that the problems she solved were answers that so many people craved. She then began teaching and helping others build what she had built. She showed them how to make it their own. It was scary at first, but the more she persevered and learned to trust herself, the more she was able to make a positive impact in the world.

By the time she was thirty-two years old, she had built a multimillion-dollar business. More importantly, she created a life that fit her unique beliefs and passions. Her work gave her days meaning, and because she took care of herself, she had the capacity to effectively care for others too. Today, she is happy, in love, and deeply connected to her purpose. She's married to the love of her life, a man who challenges her yet never lets her forget how incredibly capable she is.

I often think about these two women and how entirely different they are. They are worlds apart—and yet, I was both of them.

Betting on Myself

To rebuild my life, I had to leave everything behind. My job, my marriage, and the first house I bought. I also left behind so much resentment, anger, and self-loathing. As I packed everything I owned into a little U-Haul trailer, I began to feel a deep sense of relief and alignment. Fueled by this newfound freedom, I hopped into my Subaru Outback and headed back to my childhood home in Maryland. My eyes were set on a glimmer of hope off in the distance—the tiniest North Star there ever was.

Along the way, my favorite forest called to me. I took a season-long detour in Brevard, NC, where I split my time between a friend's couch and the woods at the bottom of my favorite mountain-bike trail. Every morning I'd go on a trail run or a mountain-bike ride on Daniel Ridge Loop in Pisgah National Forest, fueled by anger and hope for a new future. If you haven't tried a run or ride powered by fury as your life as you know it shatters around you, I highly recommend it.

I'd then return to my campsite to jump in the cold, refreshing river, the forest breathing life back into me. Every morning the river made me gasp, shocked me awake, and made my aching heart feel alive.

During the day, I read books, barefoot in a hammock. Sometimes college friends would come find me, and I would take them wading down the river, jumping off waterfalls, and sliding down natural slides—"river walking" as I liked to call it. At night, I'd build a fire and cook dinner—and as someone who is still pretty scared of the dark, this part was an especially empowering experience. I will forever be grateful for this time in my life as it was so healing. Profound rest and recovery happened in those woods. I was able to connect with myself, what I wanted, and who I was without the noise of well-meaning but generally unhelpful family and friends.

When I got back home, I told my family I was going to take the GRE, apply to graduate school, and get my PhD. I half-believed what I was telling them, but looking back now, I know I was trying to distract the curious, worried, and judging minds who wondered what came next for me. I was, ironically, leaning into a socially acceptable path even though that was precisely the thing I was trying to escape.

Why can't you bloom where you're planted?

This question created so much guilt and shame within me that I felt physically nauseous on a daily basis. I was stuck between a rock and a hard place. Being "myself" seemed to make the people in my life uncomfortable, afraid, and worried about me. But the thought of reducing myself to fit inside their "shoulds" was something I felt I could not survive.

Slowly, as I quieted the opinions of others, I was able to hear my own inner voice again. The one who knew what I wanted. The one who wasn't consumed with guilt, shame, and despair. The little voice grew louder, asking its own questions, like:

Who am I?

What do I really want in life?

How did I get here, and what will it take to get free?

How do you begin when you feel utterly broken?

Answers started to come too: *With baby steps, my dear.*

That drunk, depressed, lost girl who was so angry that the standard achievements and goals of society didn't make her happy; the one who couldn't seem to fit into the norms or feel satisfied trying; the one who drowned herself in alcohol, hoping it would all be over soon; the one who grew to hate herself, then lost her desire to go on—she was me. I think about her often, because she transformed me into the person I am today—in love with life and successful according to my own standards.

My life didn't change by some grand overnight transformation. Day after day, tiny, daily habits pulled me out of my dark pit of despair. Changing *what I did* created enough momentum that it changed my life. But *who I was* hadn't changed at all.

It's important to know that both of those people are *still* me, both the drunk and the millionaire.

The happy and fortunate soul I am today is who I've always been. I'm experiencing the joy and success that has always been inside of me. I always had access to it. I just had to take the next right baby step.

I'm Betting on You Too

If you relate to any part of my pit of meaninglessness, take some solace in knowing that you are not alone. I have a special place in my heart for those who find themselves in dark and scary places. I've been extremely blessed with a second chance at life. My days are now filled with connection, love, and purpose, and now I get to help others make those same kinds of changes. It's incredible.

If you're starting at a higher altitude than I did—good! I wouldn't wish rock bottom on anyone. But if I can build a successful life of purpose, then you definitely can too. You are also not alone, my friend. You can harness the power of baby steps and take meandering paths all along the way. Following these little curiosities can take you to unexpectedly transformative places. Even slime can have healing properties if you let it.

Let me explain.

My best friend's name is Emily, and I won't apologize for the amount of times her name shows up in this text. She's a huge part of my life, so much so that I define parts of my life as pre-Emily and post-Emily. She is also the most creative and emotionally intelligent person I've ever met and, in so many ways, a role model for me. Not just as an entrepreneur, but as a human.

Emily is brilliant and creative.

So when brilliant, creative Emily called me one day and—out of the blue—said, "I'm going to start selling slime on Instagram," my first response was a highly cautious *What the fuuuuck?* You know, that feeling when your skepticism kicks on, full throttle.

She had recently lost her mom and was struggling, so I honestly wasn't sure if it was a strange but good idea or if she was sending out a cry for help.

I was pretty sure that if she was serious, she could do it. Emily *can* do anything—but that doesn't mean I thought she *should* turn her kitchen into a slime factory.

Eyebrows raised, I listened as she explained, "People are obsessed with slime videos. My girls watch them all the time. It's an ASMR sensory thing. People find it super satisfying. There are videos about how to make it, too, but *no one* is really selling it. I think I'm going to do it!"

And she did.

Not because she had a real passion for gooey things, but because she saw an opportunity and took it.

She kept the model simple. Everything was hosted on Instagram and Shopify, with super cute and silly branding (think Melted Peeps and Narwhal Bubbles) with some genuine scarcity. The batches were always unique and had a limited quantity, which created a collector's effect that made people want to buy them all and buy them quickly.

Her girls were involved in the process, too. They'd come up with the batches together—*What would Breakfast Cereal Slime look, smell, and feel like?*—then they'd perfect the recipe and make buckets of it for the next run.

Within five months, they had their first $10,000 month. Through the holidays, they were having $1,000 days and even employed two people part-time. Not long after that, a dad who wanted to teach his daughter about entrepreneurship bought the business and supplies for $13,000, and the experiment was over just as suddenly as it started.

Here's Emily's real brilliance: when she saw an opportunity, she went for it.

She didn't overthink it. The opportunity she seized wasn't really about the market or the numbers. She wasn't looking for a passion to live out or a career to succeed in. She just needed a break from a really painful phase of life. She needed something playful to focus on with her kids instead of all the pain they were going through.

Who knew slime could be so healing?

Who knows what your "slime" could be?

I ramped up my copywriting business at the dining table of a rehab facility. I started teaching people how to build a freelance business from a coworking space in Bali. Now I'm putting the finishing touches on this book from a couch in Miami, in between sniffs of my newborn baby's delicious head (what is it about babies that smells so GOOD?).

Emily took a fun idea and a few hours a day and turned it into a way to reconnect with herself and her kids.

Wherever you are, whoever you are, I'm betting you have a business idea and an incredible future ahead of you.

I'm betting you have ideas you want to pursue and inspiration you want to chase.

I'm also betting you have doubts. You have fears. You're overwhelmed. But you're also excited, hopeful, and brave. You're brilliant and creative too, and I hope you have someone in your corner who will take your call and smile and nod while you share your wild vision.

I have no doubt that you're all of those things and more. I'm betting that when you realize just how much freedom, love, and joy you can create in your life, those mountaintop goals are only the beginning of what you can accomplish.

Even if you're not ready to make that bet yet, I will. I'll believe in you until your self-trust grows enough to believe in yourself.

CHAPTER 1

(DON'T) BET LIKE A BRO

I think we need to take some of the pressure off ourselves before we go any further, starting with the words we use.

I'll go first: *Bet on Yourself* feels a bit cliché in print. So do my program titles, Write Your Way to Freedom and Let's Build Your Online Business. And I had to squeeze my eyes shut and hit "send" when I wrote my newest business milestone into the bio for this book.

That being said, my business is thriving, and I'm an expert on the topic at hand. But when you grow up in a family where self-deprecating humor is a love language, it can be hard to own up to genuine success and expertise. I'm working on it, okay?

My entire business is to support people who are looking for a better way of life. I'm always telling people to invest in themselves—to bet on their own brilliance for a change. But when someone (myself included) referred to me and what I do in fancy schmancy business jargon, I used to straight up get the heebie-jeebies.

I know I'm not alone in this. A lot of us feel more comfortable calling ourselves "freelancers" or our businesses a "side hustle" to avoid the bro-esque connotations of "business owner," "entrepreneur," and "CEO." I caught myself resisting those terms for a long time too.

Here's where I landed: if being a bit cliché communicates more effectively and even trips the algorithm, and that brings me more people like you, I'll survive. If acknowledging my own business' growth gives someone else a glimmer of hope, I'm here for it. And if thinking of myself as a business owner or entrepreneur helps me get better at all of those things, I'll deal with the discomfort.

Not everything has to be comfortable, polished, or perfect to be good—in fact, I'd argue good work *can't* be. (Honestly, is anything all three of those, ever? And who gets to decide anyway?)

That's what made Emily's slime venture so weird *and* perfect. If you missed that part when you skipped Bet Your Bottom Dollar you might want to go back and look again. You'll need to get to know her at some point because I talk about her all the time. And her starting, running, and selling a business from her kitchen is exactly the kind of story we all need to hear.

She didn't have some five-year plan or a business-building system. She just tried a thing. Calling it a "side hustle" or a hobby wouldn't have made her any less of an entrepreneur. Actually, the fact that she was actively exchanging something she made for money meant she was more of an entrepreneur than someone who is just talking about their startup. But she also didn't take it too seriously. She remained curious, playful, and in alignment with the original purpose of her business: to find levity in the midst of a really challenging time.

What does all of this mean for you? To start, it means you might be more of an entrepreneur than you care to admit—and it also means you get to decide what entrepreneurship looks like for you.

We're about to unpack a lot of mindsets around working for yourself, but if you're still attaching "entrepreneur" and other concepts to something you don't want, you'll get stuck. A lot.

Look at it this way: you know how we use the word "literally" to mean the exact opposite of its *literal* meaning? It's the context that makes it clear. We know the difference between someone who is *literally* starving and when they're just impatiently waiting for their next meal (literally *starving*), without really thinking about it.

The same goes for becoming the entrepreneur I already know you're capable of being. The context you put around what it means to be your own boss lays the foundation for what's possible for you.

And hopefully, the context of this book is going to make it crystal clear that when you decide to bet on yourself, it's not because it's a gamble or a risk. It's because you're a better bet than almost anything else around you. When I tell you to "bet on yourself," I mean you're *literally* your own best investment.

But let's get a few misconceptions out of the way first.

Entrepreneur ≠ Bropreneur

What image comes to mind when you hear the word "entrepreneur"?

Feel free to take a moment in the bathroom, splash some water on your face, and shake off the image of all those cringey dudes with their ostentatious Twitter egos, dick rockets, and crypto envy.

While you're in there, look up at the mirror.

You're the kind of person we need running the world. The one who overthinks, cares "too much," and is deeply, sometimes cripplingly, empathetic.

Yet here we are, being taken over by bros.

The dudebro who wears black T-shirts every day to appear like he's "fighting decision fatigue" while Instagramming selfies in a rented Lamborghini like an absolute douche is not overthinking his abilities or self-worth.

If you have even a little bit more substance than that—and of course you do—I promise, the world needs you.

This may sound harsh, but I'm intentionally leaning into this bropreneur caricature because it's what dominates the images of entrepreneurs today. And I'm beyond ready for the uprising of fiercely empathetic entrepreneurs who trust themselves deeply and refuse to stay small out of fear of becoming like these bropreneurs.

Having a "testosterone-free guide" doesn't have anything to do with gender, but rather a path to being your own boss in a new era. It's time for what could be considered a more "feminine" energy in entrepreneurship.

Make no mistake, when I say testosterone-free, I'm simply referring to the metaphorical implications of this hormone. And when I say we need more feminine energy in entrepreneurship, I'm simply referring to traits that are more often associated with the feminine. Obviously, humans are beautifully complex and more dynamic than this simple dichotomy. But I digress.

What I want you to know is that embracing entrepreneurship requires embracing the discomfort of the unfamiliar. For far too long we've been living in a career landscape dominated by fear as the main motivator and unattainable productivity standards that define your worth. Not to mention the strange underlying expectation that you'll simply give the majority of your life to a company, forsaking your family without pausing to ask any questions. I'm much more interested in shifting toward conscious business practices, compassionate communication, and treating the people I work with as the whole person—remembering they are part of a family too, for crying out loud.

We need this shift if we're going to evolve. To better care for each other and the world. To create more spaces where people walk away from their jobs feeling empowered, not constantly in a state of fear.

You don't have to be a bold, risk-taking dude who gambles obscene amounts of capital or "moves fast and breaks things" to succeed. Social media and movies perpetuate this caricature because it's dramatic.

Audiences love sensational origin stories, especially when we know the big results they're leading to. But no one is Instagramming all the boring steps that come in between, which is what really creates champions.

All of the monotonous, everyday stuff gets skipped or cut into a quick montage. Who's going to watch Rocky Balboa eating three healthy meals a day, or the early days of a CEO hunched over her desk sending follow-up emails?

Here's the good news: It's the *in-between* moments—the small consistent actions—that get us to where we really want to be. If it looks like someone is jumping in feet first and risking it all to build a successful business, you probably didn't see their montage years. And although the email-sending montage might not be super sexy, it's so dang attainable that most of us miss it.

It's also important to know that you've got choices. Entrepreneurship is so varied and accessible now, we can all slide in at our own pace.

You know how it feels to slide into the pool for the first time when the water feels uncomfortably cold? You put your arms above your head, adjusting slowly until you're brave enough to dip your shoulders below the surface.

And then you turn to your friend and say, "It's not that bad."

Suddenly, you feel more comfortable in the water than out. Entrepreneurship is just like that. It's something you slide into—maybe even reluctantly at first—but before you know it, you're trying to convince your friends and family to slide in too.

"Come on in! The water's just fine!"

If your pace is slow, I'm right there with you, and so are the people I work with. Not bropreneurs, but people of all ages and backgrounds who feel overworked, underpaid, and underappreciated in their current jobs. Especially fields like nursing and teaching, which tend to wear people down.

Most people aren't fantasizing about making a billion dollars—they're just looking for a way to make good money on their own terms, without sacrificing their physical and mental health. They bet on themselves because they want to get some control back, not because they're gambling it away.

They're not draining 401(k) funds or getting venture deals. They're learning to grow their skill sets (sometimes on the side of whatever job they started in) until their confidence and income have grown enough to step out on their own.

The world doesn't need any more billionaire dudes in the space-race dick-measuring contest. But it sure as hell could use more people who are thriving, not surviving. If you'd like to live more fully, have more time for your family, be able to afford a comfortable life, and give back to the world in a meaningful way, the experience you're looking for lies outside of the prescribed nine-to-five path. And it doesn't ultimately matter if you call it entrepreneurship or not...

This is your sign to go for it.

Entrepreneurship ≠ Exclusive

The world is changing quickly, and building a business looks different than it used to.

You no longer need a brick-and-mortar location, a ton of startup capital, or machines to manufacture a product. Between the software and learning platforms available to us today, you have more access to develop your skills and build a business from scratch than ever before.

I get it though. It's one thing to say entrepreneurship is more accessible than ever before—but for so many people, it's hard to actually believe it is.

And it's something else entirely to believe that entrepreneurship is accessible to *you*.

Your relationship to the word "entrepreneur," and everything that (you think) comes with it, will be as unique as you are. But there are some generationally shared, outdated assumptions and baggage that are worth unpacking first.

Millennials (like me) were raised by Gen X (and older) parents who, for the most part, meant well. But when they were our age, they basically had one path to take in life: get a job, do good work, and provide for their family. There was no internet and very little access to anything outside of your hometown, so if you could get a degree or an advanced degree, the odds of landing a job and providing for your family were even better.

Of course, there were entrepreneurs among these generations, but only a select few. Starting a business back then meant opening a storefront, managing a team, and carrying the financial risk of everything that comes with a brick-and-mortar operation—and again, no internet—with very little guidance available. So the entrepreneurial path was limited to those who had the knowledge, resources, and risk tolerance or safety nets in place to try over and over again to make their idea work.

Entrepreneurs were admirable if they made it and reckless if they didn't. Maybe a little bit of both no matter what. Either way, it wasn't something the average (responsible) person did.

For the most part, Gen X and older lived in a world that delivered on its promises *as long as you stuck to the plan.* So their promises to us were even bigger and more hopeful than what their Depression-era parents were able to access or provide them. Everyone—from parents to high school advisors to morning episodes of *Sesame Street*—gave baby millennials the same clear, repeating message: *you can be whatever you want to be... if you stick to the plan.*

Unfortunately, their advice around *how* to access that message was heavily filtered through their limited experiences of life and success. (And again, without taking into account the impact of the internet.)

Follow your passion meant we shouldn't get any ol' job—we needed to get the *right* job.

You can do anything assumed we would get a college degree to back up those aspirations.

Be whatever you want was meant to get us excited about the world of opportunity available to us, but a lot of us felt overwhelmed by the options and expectations that came with it.

This is what we do as humans—we have an experience, and then we turn around and give advice based on our limited life experiences. *Voila! I've figured "it" out. My way is the only way.*

But we know life isn't that simple. That's why it's *so* essential you never forget you're a sovereign individual and need to take what works for you and leave the rest.

And honestly, we millennials tried to make it work. Most of us set out to follow that path by getting the degrees our parents wished they had, working in careers that were meant to create meaning, and throwing ourselves into our work.

But the world is changing, and the promise stopped delivering.

Just after we entered the workforce, the Great Recession hit. The same degrees that gave our parents a leg up on their peers left us buried in student loans for a piece of paper that many of us never really needed.

Somehow, we were supposed to discover our passion, become an expert in it, and then make a living with it, all while living a balanced life in the face of global and economic chaos.

The same jobs that people once relied on to provide for their families can now go under at any moment thanks to a series of global crises, the shorter life expectancy of businesses, and the fact that most jobs simply stopped keeping pace with our skyrocketing costs of living. And we're left reeling and confused by the turnover.

There is no safety in that strategy anymore.

We must accept this fact: for most people the path our parents had is gone.

Things are forever going to be more volatile due to rapidly changing technologies. Knowing this arms you with essential information to keep up in today's world. It's why you're truly your own best bet.

Do you still think a bimonthly paycheck from a company that barely pays you above minimum wage is more reliable than building your own online business? Tell that to the people who were suddenly deemed "nonessential" and lost their jobs in the wake of a global pandemic—without warning. It's important to differentiate between regular and reliable.

If you're not working for yourself, you're giving someone else the power to rip your income rug out from under you.

And I'm talking to millennials when I say "we" because I am one, but my students range from high schoolers to retirees. Entrepreneurship has become more accessible for my generation thanks to the internet and how quickly we adapted to it. Plus, we were kids when the dotcom dudes made their millions, and it left an impression on us, for better or worse.

It's clear that some of us have actually found a way to be anything we want to be while some of us were left behind—struggling to make sense of our outdated advice in this new world.

For the most part, it was our generation who brought the passion economy to life. Web shops and social media have made it easy for us to monetize the hobbies we turned to when our jobs just weren't enough to pay the bills or provide the meaning we're looking for.

Pre-internet, if you spent time weaving or doing pottery after work, that would be your "thing." Your job paid your bills and your hobby brought you joy. Now, you can put that pottery online, watch it take off, quit your job, and spend the rest of your life making coffee mugs from your garage if you want to. This is part of what makes entrepreneurship so accessible, and it's *definitely* a good thing.

But it's *not* so good if we get stuck thinking the way we make money must be our passion; or on the flip side if we profit off our passion, we'll taint it. It's also problematic when our parents' ideas about being an entrepreneur blind us to the new opportunities sitting right before us. Like thinking it's risky and irresponsible, or we have to go all in to eventually hit it big, or that it takes nonstop hustle and expertise to start a business.

No matter what generation we're from, or what our experiences of the workforce and entrepreneurship might be, a lot of us share similar mindset limitations. It's like we're all running a money-and-lifestyle operating system from the '80s (or before), when everything has changed around us.

It's time for an upgrade.

Who Are You Betting On?

Everything about the passion economy points to the limitations of our old paradigm. As we've tried to reconcile the old ways with new opportunities, it's no longer enough to just get a job and not enough to enjoy your spare time. If you're not all in, what are you even doing, *bruh*?

Nothing ever seems enough.

A close friend once called me for career advice and said something so relatable: "I'm just so frustrated that I'm thirty and reinventing myself *again*."

Ah, the shame around being a "jack of all trades, master of none."

For a long time, I was hung up on trying to figure out *who I was* and what my career should be. I envied the people around me who had always known they wanted to be a doctor or teacher or whatever it was and just did it. Like my friend, I wondered what it would feel like to just *know* what you wanted to do and then go do it.

Trying to find the perfect intersection of the life Venn diagram that includes what you're passionate about, what you can make money at, and where you're "supposed" to be is so intense. Couple that pressure with the whole "go to college, get a job" narrative and so many people like my friend are stuck in this cycle of getting multiple degrees, trying out a career, and starting over—or never trying anything because they think they have to stay with the career they've already invested so much time and money into.

But why?

The idea that a long, monotonous career is more valuable than one of exploration is so outdated. Most of us are never going to experience lifelong careers with companies that provide a pension. So why are we still aiming for that?

My friend has a ton of valuable skills *because* she's reinvented herself. She's a nurse and a copywriter, she's owned a charter sailing business in the Caribbean, and she's currently choosing another path. She's got so many options and choices. She's living the dream of most people, but sometimes still feels like it's not good enough.

The thing I didn't know years ago is that having a set vision for your life can be just as hard as uncertainty, especially if you feel like you have to start from the bottom to make any changes in your life. Part of this is because humans have a core desire to appear consistent. Seriously, it's a psychological phenomenon anyone in marketing or sales will share with you. But you can *choose* to push back on your programming, and instead value changing your mind, and being dynamic. This choice is incredibly empowering.

We are also hardwired to compare and contrast ourselves to everyone around us. And it can leave us constantly thinking we "should" be at a certain point of our lives *relative to the people around us* instead of thinking about where we actually want to be.

It's bullshit.

On some level, we all know it's bullshit, and yet we continue to torture ourselves with comparison.

People cannot and should not be a certain way forever. Nor should we strive to be a certain way because that's what society has told us we should be. All that gets us is an overidentification with how we make money.

Sometimes how we make money is simply how we make money.

When we give ourselves permission to change our minds, we open doors rather than letting the past dictate our future.

Making money doesn't *have* to be done with our passion—alternatively, we can use our passion to free ourselves from the constraints of the nine-to-five. And how we make money doesn't have to be the main thing that defines our contribution to the world. We already know that, yet we still define ourselves by what we do for work. It's the first question we ask when meeting someone new.

I invite you to find your next thing as many times as you need to until you love your life. Keeping in mind that what work looks like can change precisely because we have different needs depending on the season of life that we're in. And that's part of the beauty of entrepreneurship. Give yourself permission to reinvent yourself as unapologetically and often as you need until you love who you are and the life you've built.

There are many truths when it comes to creating a life you love. The key is finding what works best for *you* and not allowing "shoulds" and outdated beliefs to hold you back.

Passion (or Not), Here We Come

My generation found something out the hard way: insisting that the way we make money must also be how we define who we are can lead to major dissatisfaction. We just don't always know what to *do* with that realization. But the younger generation is figuring it out.

Gen X and millennials adapted to the internet as it emerged, but Gen Z was raised on it. We might've been shocked by the events of the last couple of decades, but Gen Z doesn't remember anything else. And because they were born into constant, rapid-fire change, they are amazing at adapting—nearly independent of their parents.

Millennials taught each other how to channel our passions into side hustles on eBay and Etsy, but Gen Z kids are going viral unboxing toys or playing video games. They don't overthink it. They just go for it.

If you are a millennial or older and don't know how accessible entrepreneurship really is, ask a Gen Z sibling or kid. They get it.

The catch is that those resources are available to all of us, not just nineteen-year-old YouTubers.

And you're no longer limited by where you're located or how much money you have. You don't even need to have a brilliant idea. All of the information, tools, and resources you could possibly need to do almost anything you can think of already exist—and since you don't have to risk much to experiment, there's no reason not to.

The biggest difference between the kids who are starting businesses now and the adults who are still just thinking about it? They don't bring as much pressure into it. *They just try.*

Specifically, they know they have permission to try new things without being an expert in them first. If you need visible examples, scroll through the live feed on TikTok, or whatever platform is relevant by the time you're reading this book. I've seen people making money there doing tarot readings, digging cross-shaped pearls out of oysters (for real), and talking about their self-care routines while people send them tips or buy their stuff.

And for every person who's making money on video platforms, there are *so many more* working behind the scenes, building a business that meets their goals with zero social media presence. Make no mistake, you do not have to be an influencer to be successful. They are just visible examples of what I'm talking about.

Do you already do something you love that can be packaged as a business? Put it on Etsy or TikTok or Instagram. Have a lucrative skill that you wouldn't mind doing a lot more of? Hone that skill, or if you're ready, grab a free website on Squarespace, watch some YouTube or Skillshare content about turning on some ads, and start looking for clients. There ya go. You're an entrepreneur.

Okay, that was massively oversimplified, and I am going to help you with more than that. But the point is that while you do need *some* resources to get started building a business, it's not tens of thousands of dollars and years of education worth. In fact, for a majority of people, studying for four years in a bubble to *then* go out and start to gain experience is a massive waste of time and resources. And oftentimes they come out into the real world with already outdated information. You see, "the path" is slow to update.

Today, the barrier to entry is insanely low. If you have a computer and internet, you're already set for the first steps. When you're ready to invest in yourself with more than just time, you can pay for services and resources that will take you further.

Entrepreneurship is more accessible than ever before, but it won't ever *feel* accessible to you as long as you're trying to find the "right" opportunity to build in the "right" way—a way of thinking that may have worked for our parents' generation but has long since become an obstacle that keeps people in a fixed mindset. As long as we keep ourselves stuck on the outdated path we started on, we'll keep spinning out over who we're supposed to be and what we think we're allowed to do.

When you're an entrepreneur, no exploration is ever truly wasted. Every lesson, every skill, every "failure" and "rejection" is all leading you where you're ultimately meant to go.

This is why you're your own best bet.

Permission to Be Yourself

Giving yourself permission is a deceptively simple concept. It encompasses a lot of mindset work. That's not to say you have to be in the perfect mindset to succeed, but working on it is going to help you get started.

Interpersonal work makes your life better all around. And when you're an entrepreneur, personal development is a top priority. You don't have to give your leftover, post-workday exhausted energy to this growth. You get to choose to prioritize your growth and reap the rewards all around.

That's why this is more a mindset book, rather than a "how to build XYZ business" book.

Gen Z (and even the bropreneurs) have made it clear that the only permission that matters is our own. The limiting beliefs we've been conditioned to have are primarily what keep us from choosing ourselves and creating opportunities.

We can access that permission whenever we want, but most of us have to get there through some kind of discomfort first. Some of us get there because we don't have another choice.

That's where Becky comes to mind. Like Emily, Becky didn't doubt herself once the opportunity to build a business became clear—mostly because she couldn't afford to.

For fifteen years she was a military wife and a stay-at-home, homeschooling mom. Then her husband left her with no warning. She had no plan and no degree or career to fall back on—she'd never even had a job before. And she had two kids to feed and a mortgage to pay.

Of course, her friends and family told her if she wanted to get a job, she should enroll in college. So she started pursuing a counseling degree, but college doesn't pay the bills while you're in classes. She realized if she stayed the course, her children would be old enough to attend college themselves before she had the income promised by a degree. That wasn't good enough; she needed money *now.*

That's when she signed up for my course, and not long after that, she decided to drop out of college. Instead, she worked her ass off cleaning houses while she learned how to be a copywriter in the thirty to sixty minutes she could squeeze out of her exhausting days.

She accumulated three months' worth of savings with her cleaning gigs and other side jobs. And then she quit cleaning houses. That gave her three months to make being her own boss full-time work.

By the time the deadline was up, Becky was making about $4,000 monthly. Soon after, she raised that number to five figures. Monthly.

In under a year, Becky went from having zero job experience to running a freelance business on her way to earning over $100,000 a year. Under the best of circumstances, she may never have earned that salary with a counseling degree—not to mention the student loans she'd have looming over her head.

Sometimes the path to inspiration isn't inspired. Failure wasn't an option, so she didn't fail.

Stress and desperation motivate us to make big changes in our lives. In fact, studies show that pressure causes real changes. Which makes sense—if life is cushy, why would we want to change?

I wouldn't wish hard times on anyone, and I'm not saying you have to be in a dark place to start a business. But I *do* think you have to be ready to make big changes in the way you think, especially when it requires you to think differently than the people around you and the way you've approached life so far. Change comes from changing how you think.

I've found that people who are at the end of their rope tend to build their businesses more efficiently because they don't have another choice. For example, my struggles with alcohol were the catalyst for the exponential growth I experienced as a person and a business owner. Similarly, Emily and Becky started their businesses not because they wanted to "be an entrepreneur," but because they needed to alleviate pain that the prescribed path couldn't touch.

Desperation can be an asset if you let it be.

That's why *amor fati* is a life philosophy for me. I even have it tattooed on my arm. Amor fati, or "love of fate," is the simple stoic philosophy that the difficulties in life are opportunities if you choose to make them so.

But that's not to say you have to be desperate to do well. You can introduce a bit of manufactured pressure. When I coach people who don't have desperate situations, I have them limit the amount of time they devote to their business. This seems counterintuitive, but if they have "all the time in the world" they end up spinning their wheels. We fill the time we allow ourselves to work on something. Certain conscious limitations actually provide focus and make our actions more effective.

If you're worried your stakes aren't high enough or your passion isn't strong enough, I have good news: when you have to show up and start the work anyway, your passion will be revealed to you along the way. You gotta show the universe that you're serious, and it will meet you halfway. I promise.

Now, if you're worried that you're *too* messed up, that you need to be *less* desperate before you can handle starting a business, I have good news: you're not, and you don't. You don't need to be whole before you start building an online business. There is healing in growth, and sometimes the personal growth that comes from starting your own business is what *helps* you heal. This is totally my story. It was my business that helped me heal. I hate to imagine where I'd be if I'd waited until I felt ready to start a business. I probably would have never started.

You don't have to hit that Venn diagram of perfect circumstances, go all in, or have a dramatic backstory to take your first steps. You just have to take them. And then take the next, and the next, growing your self-trust along the way.

You don't have to be Becky, Emily, or me any more than you have to be a bropreneur.

Your story is your own.

If all you can see is how different you are from us, it's that torturous comparison talking. Push back. The best way to use this book (or any book, honestly) is to look for similarities instead of differences. Don't forget to look extra close when something feels uncomfortable, too. Meaningful change is found in that place of discomfort.

Ask yourself, *How can I relate in a way that teaches me something? How can I squeeze the most value out of this?*

Emily needed to find a bright spot in a dark time, even if it didn't turn into a lifelong business or multimillion-dollar venture. In fact, she didn't want either of those things.

Becky needed to feed her kids *now*, even if it didn't look like the typical path to a career. In fact, the typical path would've left her and her kids in an even bigger mess than they were in.

I simply needed to not hate my life.

None of our stories were glamorous.

We only found our way through because we let ourselves try something new and embrace the discomfort that comes with that territory.

Place Your Bets

Books are such a funny middle ground between sharing stories and having a conversation. What I'd really love to do right now is sit down on the couch and talk with you. I have *so* many questions for you. Like a whole list of them. So I'll share some of them now. But be real: even if I asked you to answer them one at a time, you're just going to skim through them, aren't you?

Your brain is itching to jump ahead and figure out the "right" answer to each of them (*hint* there is no *right* answer).

And that's if you even stick around to read them.

I could make this book a million pages long, with all kinds of page breaks and dividers and

GIANT

CALLOUT

TEXT

just to get your attention and help you keep pace.

But the most helpful tool I've found in this life is answering thoughtful questions. It's up to you to decide if you want to play along—if you trust that this is helpful for you too—and maybe you'll get something out of it.

If you really want to get the most out of the questions in these sections, grab a piece of paper and a notebook, and let's play.

Take special note of your initial knee-jerk response to the questions. In the moment just after reading the question and before your conscious mind manufactures a curated answer, you have a window of radical honesty and transparency. Grab on to those because they are clues.

We'll start with the easy ones:

What are three things you wish you could change about your life right now?

Maybe it's not worrying about money all the time, wishing you could pay off student loans, having more time with your kids, being able to afford organic groceries without worrying about the bill... Maybe you just want something to look forward to.

What are three things you wish you could do more of in your life?
Maybe it's traveling more, working less, creating more, making music, dancing, or spending time with family.

What life changes would allow you to do more of the things you love and less of the things you don't?
Maybe it's earning more while working less, finding remote work, moving to a different place, or having time to work out or cook more meals.

Do you already have a hobby, passion, skill, or interest that you could develop into a business?

What thoughts and feelings come up for you when you think about making money from that?

Do you experience resistance to the idea of selling something you create or provide? Write out some of the exact thoughts you have around the idea of profiting off of your passion.

Now, we're getting somewhere:

How do you identify with your work or work history?
Have you caught yourself saying things like "Charging what I'm worth"? Do you feel proud of your job?

Ashamed? Do you avoid talking about how many times you've "reinvented" yourself?

What comes up for you when you think about blue-collar and white-collar work? Do you think money has to be earned through hard work or a certain kind of work?

What kind of work did your parents or caregivers do? What did their experiences teach you about what is and isn't possible around work and careers? *Maybe you had a dad who worked sixty hours every week, yet never seemed to have enough, so you learned that the only way to get by is by working endlessly. Or maybe you had a mom who brought home plenty of money, so you had everything you wanted, but she was hardly ever around. So, you learned that to be financially successful, you have to sacrifice time with your family. (What you learned isn't "good" or "bad," and it doesn't make your family wrong. We're all doing the best we can.)*

Okay, some easy ones again:

Name three entrepreneurs that first come to mind.

What traits do these people have?

Now, name three people you're closest to in your life.

Imagine telling them you're going to start a business. How would they react?

Let's circle back real quick:

> **Where can you find evidence of the traits listed above in your own life?**
> **And when you made your list of entrepreneurs, did you go with the obvious? The quintessential?**
> *Can you go a little deeper? Don't forget, the lady who runs your salon or yoga studio is an entrepreneur. The stands at the local farmers' market are owned by entrepreneurs.*

This one's the hardest. Ready?

> **How do you feel after answering those questions?**

A lot of fear, judgments, questions, and doubts might be coming up for you right now. When we try something new, say a hobby or skill, it's understandable to expect a certain amount of awkwardness and discomfort until you get the hang of it. The same thing is true for trying a new way of thinking. So, if you're feeling some discomfort, that's okay. We've got time to get the hang of this.

CHAPTER 2

DON'T TRADE YOUR OLD BOSS FOR A WORSE ONE

After I had worked for myself for several years, I was ready for what I thought was the next step. Being able to take vacations when I wanted was a nice part about having my own business. Being able to work while I traveled seemed even cooler because that meant I could be gone longer and worry less about saving for a trip. But what I *really* wanted was to be completely location-independent. The digital nomad lifestyle appealed to me, and Bali looked like the place to try it.

A lot was happening in my life leading up to that trip. A three-year relationship was very obviously coming to a close. A major portion of my income disappeared overnight when I had to walk away due to some…ethical misalignment (more on that whole mess next chapter).

Long story short, I was in another season of change, and I thought Bali would be the culmination of everything I had been working toward. Without any set return time, I was going to live the dream: work near a beautiful beach and make great connections with like-minded people while growing my business, my new course, and my community. I imagined using my awesome experiences there to show my students what life could be like for them when they built their own businesses (without coming off braggy or influencer-y, of course).

It didn't take long to realize my expectations did not match reality.

Being Your Own (Worst) Boss

Sure, Bali was beautiful—in the moments when I actually saw it. After taking calls at an ungodly hour with people in US time zones, I would just keep working, feeling pressure to hold a nine-to-five schedule for fear of others thinking I was screwing around on a tropical island.

By "others" I mean my clients, students, friends, and family—you know, the ones who were all back in the States and had no real way of actually monitoring (and therefore judging) me.

And by "nine-to-five" I mean before the sun came up until after it went down again.

Some of my overwork came from how badly I wanted my business to look "valid." I came from a family full of "noble" professions like finance, science, or law. Degrees were a measure of success, and my degree was collecting dust on a shelf. Even though I had been my own boss for years by that point, I was always low-key worried they were judging me. Mostly because they didn't understand this new online world. Remember, this was pre-pandemic. They couldn't reconcile that meaningful work could happen remotely, like from the beaches of Bali. So I tried to demonstrate it to them by the number of hours I spent working.

Ironically, the other thing that kept me stuck in front of my laptop in a coworking office longer than most (shoutout to the few others who were there as long as I was—I hope you've found some peace too) was that my work actually *was* meaningful.

Not only did I love my clients, but thanks to the program I had just launched, a ton of people were suddenly relying on me. I felt tremendous pressure and desire to not let them down. Before then, I could just knock out client tasks at any hour of the day. Now, I had students to monitor and connect with. I would have been mortified if they thought I wasn't taking my mentorship role seriously.

These were the stories I told myself while working to the point of burnout, all while living in the gorgeous place I had told myself was going to finally give me what I wanted from being my own boss. But not even Bali is an escape when the person you're running from is yourself.

The Stories We Tell Ourselves

All of that judgment I perceived came from others was really me subconsciously judging myself. Constantly. And god, it felt lonely.

On top of caring way too much about the perceived expectations of faraway people and their (my) impossible standards, I wasn't connecting with the kind of people I was hoping to meet. Sure, I met a few cool people who were doing meaningful work. But the rest were either brand-new to entrepreneurship, or drop-shipping bros who had an ego about how they had hacked the system, all while building their brands on the backs of the same people they would call stupid or sheep for working in factories or offices all day long. At least they gave me a direct outlet for all that judgment, I guess.

At the time, I didn't realize how much judgment was consuming me. I didn't realize how much fear was behind it, either—or that I was really searching for meaning. I didn't realize how important it was for me to build community and commit to growing something that had genuine and measurable impact until Bali fell apart.

Actually, it's more accurate to say that I fell apart in Bali.

It had been years since I'd had a panic attack. Turns out, leaving a long-term relationship, trying to grow my business in a brand-new way, taking on students, obsessively worrying about their success, and being alone in a foreign country with just my own misguided expectations to keep me going is just the right combination. Fuel, meet fire.

The more I tried to use work to bury my anxiety, self-doubt, and insecurities, the more it all dragged me down.

I knew enough about what a panic attack felt like to know exactly what was happening when it hit, but I also knew that I needed help to get through it—and there was no one to call. It was the middle of the night for anyone at home that I would've otherwise called. I hadn't made deep enough friendships with any digital nomads I had met. Surprise, surprise, it was hard to connect with transient people who worked as much as I did or who ran around grabbing photos of their coconut water for the Gram, or even the few who were actually living my dream. Not enough to call them in this scenario.

I went to Bali to be immersed in a new way of living, but I wound up carrying so much of my old beliefs with me that I snapped. My strongest memory of that trip is the bathroom floor where I collapsed under the weight of my own stories.

Working for yourself really is the dream—until your new boss treats you like shit.

If you're quitting your job to escape an awful boss, what's the point if you're just going to hold yourself to those same broken standards?

Everything I said in the last chapter still stands—you should definitely ditch the crappy boss, as fast as you can or as slowly as you need to. But you also have to treat yourself better once you do break free.

And that has to start with the stories you tell yourself about what makes up your self-worth and what freedom even looks like.

What Got You Here Won't Get You There

The problem wasn't Bali, really. It was my mindset. I wasn't acting like a business owner; I was acting like an employee. The criticisms and pressures playing out in my head were those of a micromanaging boss expecting me to work forty-plus hours or more every week for the good of the company (ugh, just typing that feels gross).

I had been out of that environment for years, but I hadn't actually let those expectations go.

I still sat down at a desk from nine to five and filled all of those hours with tasks. That's how things got so out of hand in Bali. I had rigid expectations of what work and success looked like, and ultra-high expectations of how I should or could help my clients and students. I didn't want to turn down anyone's call at whatever hour was convenient for them, and once I was there for a predawn call, I might as well stay for breakfast, and then through lunch, and oh look, more to do until evening...

It's an easy trap to fall into.

When it's your business, working nonstop doesn't feel the same as putting in unpaid overtime for a boss who doesn't give a shit about you. Working for yourself can carry more meaning, so it can be seriously difficult to enforce healthy boundaries.

Especially when you really need to set those boundaries with yourself. It's a lot like quicksand. When there's always work to be done, when do you stop?

I don't know about you, but a big reason I became an entrepreneur was that working forty hours a week didn't appeal to me. I'd seen how people spent the last hours of the day and week wasting time just to run out the clock, and it was painfully illogical to me to wait around just to hit an arbitrary amount of time. Wouldn't it make more sense to incentivize efficient work so we could all go live our lives? But I hadn't fully navigated that mindset yet, so the hours I worked became one of many manifestations of "shoulds" that controlled my Bali days and pressured me to live a lifestyle I never wanted. I got sucked into tasks I knew weren't necessary to be successful, like constantly posting on social media, responding instantly to clients, and chasing the most recent trend.

There were all these boxes that I thought I had to check to be legitimate, even if they weren't necessary to my business. But without naming and going after what I truly wanted, all I had were the traditional beliefs of what work "should" look like. My old beliefs and new beliefs were complete contradictions...and it was showing.

Bali wasn't in line with what I wanted—and I couldn't even see that until I hit the floor.

So what *did* I think I was getting out of the trip?

The obvious answer is the digital nomad lifestyle. It looks like total freedom, and for people who are just breaking out of the rat race for the first time, it can be.

But I'd already experienced the novelty of extensive travel by then, and just "working in a new place" wasn't really what I wanted. I actually wanted the freedom of getting to choose my commitments—control over my location, yes, but also my schedule and my workload.

I already had a taste of that control when I quit a massive contract that felt misaligned. How often do you get to just leave when your job doesn't feel like a good fit anymore? I was also meeting a long-time goal by finally being able to take that long trip, which felt awesome. And all of that stood in serious contrast to the never-ending task load I felt chained to every hour of every day I was there.

I also realized I craved a community of people who shared my values. I thought being surrounded by entrepreneurs would be enough, but it wasn't. It felt like a sham. Part of me even felt tricked.

While I thought I was chasing freedom, I realized I was chasing a collection of experiences. It takes time and commitment to build something meaningful. Bali helped me realize that there is freedom in duty and responsibility to a community. When you show up for others consistently, you are able to grow something truly impactful. Impact is what makes a successful, lasting business. And a successful business is really what gives you freedom. What an honor.

While I still wouldn't go back long term (probably), it wasn't Bali or the digital nomad lifestyle that was the problem. It was all the beliefs I took with me when I went.

We've grossly intertwined our self-worth with our work. The work model we've been conditioned to has a way of making us forget our true desires entirely. It's so ingrained in us that even when we do step out on our own, without anyone else managing our days or making our business decisions, we still fill our heads with stories of "shoulds" that block out the "whys" that inspired us in the first place.

I did have to build a certain level of freedom to learn these lessons. It took years of hard work to wind up there, at a place I thought was going to be my ultimate destination. All too often we think we know what we want, and it keeps us grinding away with a low buzz of dissatisfaction humming in our ears. Sometimes we have to get there to realize it's not what we want. But sometimes we can learn and avoid pain by hearing other people's stories. So if you can learn from my story, the lesson here is this: get back in touch with what you *really* want or the desires that existed before the conditioning around careers took over. If you can work to see where old mindsets might be standing in your way, then you'll find the keys to a more meaningful life. Next will be mustering the courage to take your next step in the right direction.

And at the very least, maybe we can stave off a panic attack on the other side of the world.

Chasing Your Dream

Last chapter, we talked about how weird it can feel to call ourselves entrepreneurs even when the possibilities are all right there at our fingertips. But we haven't talked about what makes us want to go after it anyway, even when it sounds intimidating.

As important as it is to believe entrepreneurship is possible for you, it's just as essential to connect with the desire that tells you to give it a shot.

And usually, it's just as much about a desire to get away from what isn't working as it is about creating something new.

Working hourly sucks, especially if you're not happy with the value you get for those hours. The corporate world (healthcare, education, finance, or wherever else you're coming from) might give you an "essential" job that sounds good in theory, but if you can't ask for time off when something comes up with your family or mental health, and the working environment is shitty the rest of the time, you're going to burn out eventually.

As unglamorous as it is, my very first goal as an entrepreneur was to just not hate my life.

I always struggled to fit into traditional career choices. Every iteration of school and work I tried before becoming an entrepreneur felt too narrow in one way or another.

Becoming your own boss gives you control over everything. This immediately appealed to me, though I was simultaneously terrified.

As a business owner, you decide your schedule, your work capacity, your location, your environment, and your coworkers. You choose what you do, who to help, and what to make. Your rates, your deadlines, your services…

That kind of freedom simply doesn't exist when you're an employee. As an employee, your boss controls your day. As an entrepreneur, you spend your time as you see fit.

That level of freedom doesn't even feel real when you first start imagining it.

In fact, it's actually hard to know what it feels like to have that kind of freedom before you find yourself in it. And once you do, you may even find it overwhelming at times. Like how I would feel bad or lazy when I wasn't working forty hours, but my partner was. Or how I'd feel ashamed when my friends asked if I really worked—because I was traveling so much. But once you acclimate to that level of freedom, you'll never want to go back.

The desire to be in control of your income and your time can absolutely be enough to get started. You don't have to dream big right away.

Just *the idea of maybe someday* working from Bali can be enough. Or even being able to afford adding avocado to your sandwiches (hey, that was one of my first goals). And some of us might need to end up in a panic attack to realize we want more...but we all have to start somewhere.

Chasing the dream doesn't mean you have to have a master plan right now. Sometimes it just means you're taking steps toward alleviating pain until you're ready to dream bigger.

What are some bite-sized dreams that you have?

My list used to include "add avocado without thinking about it costing extra" and "work somewhere without fluorescent lighting."

Spend some time writing out the little things you'd like to achieve. You'll be amazed at how quickly those dreams start to come true (and how good it'll feel when they do!). Here are some from my students to get you started:

To buy myself a new wardrobe that isn't full of holes/stuff I've had for years.

To be able to buy my husband and family Christmas and birthday presents.

To buy all the fountain pens and inks I want without financial limitations.

To never have to ask for permission to go on vacation again.

To never have to go to work and come home in the dark during winter.

To have a window in my office.

To be able to go to the bathroom when I want. (I was shocked to learn this is one teachers and nurses struggle with!)

To have time for my typewriter poetry without the "you should be working" feeling.

To avoid traditional phone calls. (I don't mind Zoom or Google Meet calls but ugh, phone calls actually make me physically nauseous/migraine-y! I can't explain it, but I blame my anxiety and the "on call any time" life of a counselor and teacher.)

To be able to donate to my church and the charities that touch my heart.

To sit with a friend in need right when they need it, not "after I get off work."

To be able to work in a way that accommodates my neurodivergence—breaks whenever I need them, minimal interruptions, minimal spontaneous social situations to navigate, being able to control my routines and adjust my work environment to be more sensory friendly—lower light, noise-canceling headphones, etc.

To be able to say, "I did it."

Add yours!

Sometimes, the Dream Chases You

It makes perfect sense to set your goals on smaller dreams because our brains don't like big, fast changes. We have all kinds of biases that kick in to "protect us" when change is happening. That means, most likely, the thing standing between you and realizing that dream is the same thing driving the loops and patterns that have kept you where you are now. And that, my friend, is your mindset.

The word "mindset" is deceptively simple and wildly overused, but it's incredibly important. These two syllables hold a lot of nuanced potential. All of our preconceptions, conditioning, and programming fit in mindset, some (many) that we aren't even fully conscious of. (I don't want to get all conspiracy theory on you, but the mindset that working hard for some company is virtuous while working on your own terms is irresponsible or risky has kept a lot of money and power in the hands of a small group of people for a very long time.)

And no, I'm not going to gaslight you into thinking you're the *only* thing in your own way. Mindset is a big part of being able to build a business, but it's still just one part of it. There could be *a lot* of other things you have to work through. Physical, socioeconomic, financial, and a whole host of other contributing factors pose greater challenges for some than others. The difference is, if you remove those other obstacles but still have an employee or scarcity mindset, you'll never really get where you want to go.

I'm also not being glib when I say mindset is the most important part of building a business. Mindset encompasses all of the habits we need to break, fears we need to work through, and judgment we need to detach from. It helps you gain clarity around your desires. It brings better self-awareness, and so much more resilience than you realize you have the capacity for—mindset work really does encompass almost everything you need to create the life you want. It's the difference between finding freedom and becoming yet another bad boss you can't escape.

Let's break down some of the mindsets that can keep us stuck, even when we're more than ready for freedom.

Limitations: "But I Can't..."

Have you ever thought, *I can't do that-thing-I'm-really-interested-in-doing because I'm not qualified*?

Maybe we don't feel qualified or responsible enough to be a business owner, so we think of ourselves as "freelancers." That term *feels* much safer than "entrepreneur," but in reality, they are one and the same.

Maybe we're afraid we won't be able to learn the logistics of running a business, or we convince ourselves that we have to learn everything there is to know before we can take the next step, so we keep our dreams small.

Maybe no one ever handed us a piece of paper that said we were qualified, so we never stepped out at all.

None of those expectations reflect reality. If you're good enough for people to pay you for your product or service, you're good enough to start your own business doing it. Period. We already know that; we just don't *know* it.

This blew my mind when I started my event planning business. Prospective clients looked at my Instagram to see some of the photos from events I'd planned, asked me questions about my ideas for what they wanted, and then cut me a check to make the event happen. That's it. They didn't know me at all and just...handed me their money. I'll never forget the time one of my first clients wrote me a check for $40,000. It was wild! That was the exact same amount as the annual salary from my last nine-to-five. I'd never seen so much money all at once before. I went on to give it my all and pull off a massive event for over five hundred people—the governor included. It was even published in a magazine. I was so proud of this event mostly because I figured it out as I went. I didn't have a degree in event planning; I simply started with smaller events and got bigger and bigger each time. I came up with ideas and gave myself enough time to figure it out, asking questions along the way. Each experience gave me so much confidence for everything I would decide to do after that.

Today, I run an online business and teach others how to do the same—but I don't have an English degree. I didn't have any background in marketing before I started. And I would never have made it this far if I'd waited to become an expert before starting my business. I learned as I went, as a writer and as an entrepreneur. And yes, that includes the seemingly scary details, like how to start an LLC, set aside a percentage of income for taxes, and buy your own health insurance.

Bropreneurs have perpetuated the myth that it's difficult to start a business, but in a country literally built for entrepreneurs, it's not difficult to get the legal stuff taken care of. You can apply for an LLC through your state's Secretary of State website, purchase your own healthcare through your state's exchange, and fork over a couple hundred (tax-deductible) bucks for an accountant to file your taxes for you in April. Boom. You're a legal, legitimate business owner who doesn't need an employer.

The point isn't that I have all the answers when it comes to starting a business, but that *you* can find whatever answers you need, whether it's a detail about business building or a skill that'll help you serve your clients and customers better. The solutions you need are out there; you just have to remind yourself that millions of people have figured it (whatever "it" is) out before you, and you can figure it out too.

Even more than that, it's okay to not know everything before you get started. You truly can figure it out as you go.

You can get started with so much less than you think you need. Trust me, we've all been there, and most of us have left breadcrumbs for you to pick up along the way. There are answers everywhere. You just need to stay open-minded and ready to receive them. I promise.

Perceptions: "But I'll Look like..."

Here's another fun bit of conditioning most of us got: this idea that owning a business is "risky" and working a wage job is "safe." Which naturally means leaving a job looks unsafe;

being an entrepreneur looks reckless. Job, good. Business owning, bad. You can literally hear the black-and-white, reptilian-brain thinking here.

There may have been a time when this was true—but if the Great Recession maimed the idea of the stable day job, COVID-19 destroyed it once and for all. If you still believe being employed is the safest bet, look around at all the evidence that points to the contrary.

I remember going to a keynote by Peter Diamandis well before the pandemic, where he talked all about the future and how abundant, inspiring, and exciting it was...*because* technology was changing rapidly. *Because* companies weren't going to last as long. And *because* the world was going to be completely different. He was talking about change as a good thing, but it freaked people out because change is scary. I latched on to it so hard that I emailed him to get a copy of the slides.

That's how I was operating before 2020: Companies don't last as long as they once did, *so we're our own best investment.* Whatever skills we can acquire, whatever work we can do for ourselves *is* the safe bet. Then the pandemic hit, and students in my course started sharing stories about how they were grateful to only have lost one client but not their entire income, or how suddenly they were the breadwinners because their spouses lost their jobs, or how they were relieved they could work from home with their kids. And it all came rushing back.

Peter totally called it: there is no such thing as a safe job in the twenty-first century.

Maybe it's just too scary to face the quiet fear that any job can be taken away at any time, but even if we take the pandemic or the Recession out of the equation, plenty of states hold the legal right to fire employees for any reason they want.

Others could restructure, run layoffs, or change your role at any given moment.

But that doesn't have to be a scary thing.

So (if you really don't want to be reckless), is putting your whole livelihood in the hands of someone else really the way to go?

Recklessness isn't the only perception that holds us back though. Women, especially, tend to worry about being perceived as greedy for wanting more. Plenty of my students who started earning more than their husbands got to hear them say "Now I can quit my shitty job and look for something better!" But until you're up against that scenario, all you can do is imagine how someone might respond. The off chance that it will cause conflict in your marriage or that you'll somehow be misunderstood can feel loud. And when *that* perception of *their possible* perception changes *your perception* of your options... Can you see how much this work is rooted in mindset?

So often our fears are about things that haven't even happened yet, which means the call came from inside the house.

If you're the one worried about being greedy...

If you're the one afraid of being irresponsible...

If you're the one who doesn't perceive yourself as qualified...

Then it doesn't matter what other people do or don't say. You have to deal with those concerns within yourself first because you're the one who has to live your life.

It's time to find confidence for yourself, inside of yourself—if the people in your life don't start out supportive, they will come around. Once they see the joy, peace, and happiness you're cultivating by betting on yourself over and over again, they'll be happy for you too. And if not, you've outgrown them, and you will go on to survive and thrive beyond that pain as well.

And yeah, we'll get into that more later, too.

Hesitation: "But What if..."

Fear is an extremely powerful thing. Really, it's the one mindset obstacle that underlies all the others. It drives most of our conditioning, informs most of our perceptions, and justifies all of our limitations.

And we hate looking directly at it. All of our "what ifs," "I can'ts," and excuses sound convincing when we're using them to rationalize inaction. For example, most people I've talked with will tell me they don't want to take the risk of entrepreneurship because they're afraid of failing. Sounds reasonable, I guess. But honestly? I call bullshit.

Define "fail" for me. Have you ever done that? What does it mean to fail? You're not taking on some kind of venture capital obligation here, and I'm not asking you to make some all-or-nothing leap of faith that means losing everything if your big idea doesn't work. That's some bropreneur shit.

You can keep your current job and start a side hustle way before turning it into a full-on business. You can go slow and ease into entrepreneurship at your own pace. So what does failing even mean in that case—getting some time back to regroup around what you've learned? What's failing if you've already quit your job—going back into your old industry?

The worst-case scenario here is literally ending up right back where you are now.

That means you're already in it. The longer you keep yourself stuck, the longer you're living out your worst-case fears. If you're not scared enough to leave your current situation, then there's no reason to be scared of ending up back in it.

I'm not saying "failing" doesn't sting. No one wants the disappointment and embarrassment of saying you're going to do something and it not panning out. But you know what?

Be brave enough to let others see you trying. You've "failed" at something before, with a lower potential upside than this, and you made it through.

This brings us to the deeper layer here, and all the way back to our desires: I think often the real fear people have is of success.

Just as failure has more emotions than imagery behind it, so does success. Many of us struggle to visualize what it would even mean to succeed. When you don't know what success can look like for you—especially when you can't access what you want anymore—it's easy to fall on excuses to avoid facing the unknown.

If you told me when I started this journey that my business would become a team of twenty-one people serving thousands of students, pulling eight figures a year, and making the Inc. 5000 list, I would have laughed.

I wouldn't have believed my business could grow that much, and even if it did, Past Sarah wouldn't have even wanted it. I didn't have the mental capacity to imagine, let alone handle, the pressures of that kind of business. What if I couldn't keep it up? What if all those people were counting on me, and I stopped succeeding and let them down? I can see the obsessive spirals playing out as I write this—I just wanted to hate my life less, not take on the responsibility of people's livelihoods. The responsibility would have overwhelmed me.

Every time I hit a new level of growth, fear shows up, and I hesitate. But I'm not panicking anymore. I know I can learn anything I need to learn and ask the questions I need to ask, and I am always gaining more confidence and seeing myself in a better light, and that makes "What if...?" an exciting question, not a scary one.

It's okay to hesitate sometimes while you face something new. Just don't stay stuck there. You've got a dream to build.

Let's get this all out in the open, shall we? Grab your notebook and make three lists:

1. "But I can't..." thoughts
2. "But I'll look like..." thoughts
3. "But what if..." thoughts

Notice what thoughts come up for you and jot them down. Pay special attention to which ones come up first, rather than the thoughts your mind curates. And of course, feel free to venture outside of these initial prompts. This simple yet impactful process cultivates greater self-awareness, and that, my friend, is an essential practice on this journey.

Waking Up to Possibility

I don't want you to get the wrong idea. Reading about my life and hearing me pump you up won't change your outlook on work and business building. Not overnight, anyway.

Our beliefs are reinforced through our perception of our experiences over and over again, and it's going to take time and repetition to break down limiting beliefs and replace them with empowering ones. But naming what you're actually up against—both what you're afraid of *and* what you really want—is the first step toward changing your mindset and shifting your path toward the life you want to build. This is such a simple step (though not the easiest) that people often skip it.

When things get uncomfortable, our response is often to not deal with it. We ignore the problem and hope it will go away. But it's never really out of sight, out of mind. We can always see it on the edges of our peripheral vision, looming in the shadows like an imaginary monster following our every move, waiting for the perfect chance to leap.

That monster, made up of all the "shoulds" and stories we tell ourselves, keeps us small. It's the constant threat of some unnameable outcome that holds a ton of power *as long as we let it stay in the shadows.* As soon as we drag that monster into the light and face it head-on, we realize it's something we can deal with. In fact, we usually realize it's just a piece of us, an unmet need, a dream from our childhood, a story we adopted from one of our parents that isn't actually ours to keep. And we see it's not all that scary anyway.

That doesn't mean you have to not be afraid before you can act. If you wait for that, you'll be waiting way too long. Confidence comes from taking action. You just have to find enough courage to take the next right step despite the fear.

So let's look at the fears we just talked about to see how we can turn them into possibility.

From "But I Can't..." to "If They Can, I Can"

Say it with me: "My struggles aren't unique."

Okay, I know that sounds kind of harsh, but hear me out. Everything has pretty much been done before, right? Like, literally everything. It doesn't matter how unique your struggle feels; someone else has had it too, or something close to it. But that's a good thing.

That means someone has struggled with the exact same fears you're having right now. Someone has survived and thrived beyond whatever you're facing.

Someone has overcome your fears, learned your lessons, and developed the skill you want to have—and I guarantee they've left breadcrumbs for you to pick up along the way.

The answers won't all live in one person's experience, but if you're feeling unqualified for any reason at all, there is no way you're alone. There's a course to take, an article to read, or a mentor to connect with. You will find someone who's been where you are.

Start pushing back on the idea that you need a higher level of education to be successful. Push back on the limitation that you have to know more before you go after what you want. You have access to everything you need, right now.

And remember not to worry too far into the future. In three months, Future You will not be the same person as Present You. Future You is more knowledgeable, more experienced, and more capable—even if ever so slightly. They say "Life is short," and that's not wrong, but time is weird, and I prefer to remind myself that life is also really long. So allow Present You to make today's decisions and leave future decisions to Future You. Don't try to figure it all out now. Growth is a slow play. Give yourself permission to let it unfold.

From "But I'll Look..." to "Looks Aren't Everything"

I can't say it enough: at the end of the day, the only perception that matters is yours. But even if an outside-in perspective did matter, you're not doing anything wrong here. If you still think you'll look "bad" for wanting out of the nine-to-five, just remember greed is hoarding billions of dollars of wealth and evading taxes while exploiting people for labor.

Not wanting to struggle anymore or hoping you might one day be able to be more generous is not greedy. You're fine. In fact, we need more people like you to live a life beyond survival. We need you thriving because you're exactly the kind of person who is going to turn around and help the next person up.

And anyway, would you rather look productive and be miserable or forget about looks and just be happy? That's what I thought.

Try hanging on to thoughts like these instead: *I don't need to work eight hours a day to be successful or responsible*; *I'm actively untying my time from how much I earn, and what I'm producing is not the same as my personal value*; and *I am not how I earn money*.

From "But What if..." to "What if I Can?"

Here's the truth about all of this: there is someone out there "less qualified" than you doing what you want to do and thriving. So there's no reason not to try.

I'm not shaming you here. Totally the opposite. I want you to really know that you're not alone. That you already have what it takes to be a wildly successful entrepreneur.

That you deserve to not hate your life. Love your life, really.

That you don't have to stay stuck in survival mode, and that once you finally do break out of it, your amazing, generous, kind, big-dreaming self is going to shine as you were always meant to shine.

That you don't have to have all the answers—you just have to show up. And when you do show up, a whole community of us will be waiting for you, cheering you on, and helping you along.

The most important, all-encompassing advice I can give you is to handle any problems, fears, and limiting beliefs as they come up. Not in a reactive way, but just go with the flow. Overplanning is a recipe for inaction. If something isn't an immediate issue, table it. That's a problem for Future You. Focus on finding the best way to address your immediate obstacles—because there's always a way around them. And on the other side of those obstacles, the dream that you're chasing gets so much bigger than you can even imagine.

Now it's time to round out the lists we made earlier. If more limitations came up for you as you kept reading, go ahead and add them. The point of this exercise is to find clues to the contrary. Let's begin.

1. **Transform your "I can't..." into "If they can, I can":** go back through each and see if you can dispute them, one by one, with evidence of other people who figured it out (just like you have and will). Bonus points if you find a story from your own life that proves to you that you can do it.

   Example: "I can't figure out new tech" becomes "I'm practicing becoming more tech-savvy. I figured out how to use my new printer and install new software. I have evidence that I can figure out new tech and will continue to do so!"

2. **Shift "But I'll look..." to "Looks aren't everything":** for each item on this list, write an alternative thought that is fueled by a determination to do it anyways. Write as if you

were talking to a dear friend and encouraging them to see past their doubts.

Example: "But I'll look irresponsible" becomes "I trust in my own reliability and know that I am a more responsible bet than my current situation. It may take others time to come around to my idea, but I'm not going to let their discomfort stop me from moving forward."

3. **Reframe "What if…":** name empowering, rational alternatives to each of your what-if thoughts. You can, and you will!

   Example: "What if I am a complete failure and end up broke and homeless!" becomes "There are a lot of steps between here and being destitute. I trust myself to check in, learn from my mistakes, and course correct along the way."

Making Space for New Stories (and Bigger Dreams)

So naming what you want brings up some excuses and fears, and facing them gives you the opportunity to reframe and work around them (a.k.a. to do mindset work). Then doing that work gives you access to new ideas and bigger actions you can take, which uncovers new desires and, get this, more fears. It's a beautiful cycle of challenges, discoveries, experiments, iterations, and growth. And this perpetual cycle of growth doesn't ever have to stop! You get to choose how far the limit is.

Now that we know what we're up against (and that it's going to involve us repeatedly facing our fears and growing into stronger versions of ourselves), let's try dreaming again. Not just about what you're escaping. Really think about what you could do with your success as an entrepreneur.

I'll go first.

After Bali, I listened to the warning sign of that panic attack and changed how I worked. I stopped holding myself to traditional working hours, and as a rule, I haven't worked a forty-hour-plus week since then. Of course, there are times when the hustle creeps back in, but I simply course correct, and I try to get back to what I know works best for me.

I also don't expect my team to work long hours. In fact, I am always structuring their work, so as they get better and faster at their role, they get to reap the rewards of finishing early. Walk away! Enjoy your life! The team of twenty-one people that I would've been terrified to manage before are now my go-to people, and it's my favorite thing to give them paid maternity leave, higher pay, or time off when their world falls apart.

They are the community I never found in Bali.

And so is my family.

I wish I could take you back to the moment my family saw how many people showed up to my first annual event. They were all the same students I'd worked with for months, but it made them real to my family. They could see the legitimacy of my work that they'd been looking for in a degree or familiar job title. Priceless.

One of the moments that confirmed entrepreneurship as the only option for me forever was my granddad's ninetieth birthday. He was one of the most important people in my life.

My family all got together on the shore in Maryland to celebrate with him. But while my siblings, cousins, aunts, and uncles all struggled to get time off from work, I just booked a flight. When everyone else rushed to get back to work, I got to stay as long as I wanted. I had a whole week with just my granddad and grandma. I suspected this time was a gift, but I didn't know just how precious it was until he passed away a few months later.

I had counted down to Bali for so long, but this was the kind of freedom I was actually craving. To be with my granddad on his birthday. To be able to afford sailing lessons for weeks beforehand so I could take him out for the first time in five years. Sailing was his passion, and I was able to take him out his very last time. To help give him access to his passion, his dream, when he didn't think it would ever happen again—this is the gift entrepreneurship has given me.

For me, the dream realized was to be with my sister so she wouldn't give birth alone, and to stay with her for a month afterward while she settled in with my amazing nephew. To stay and help my friend when she had twins and her husband had next-to-no paternity leave. To pay for my friend's children's private school as she navigated a nasty divorce, so their world wouldn't be turned upside down. To become the boss who encouraged a family-centered life—for me *and* my team.

To be generous. To believe in abundance. To actually *be* a good person, after so many years believing bullshit stories about how many hours a "good" person has to work.

That's what building my own business has meant to me.

That's what I'm chasing more of—for me and you and anyone else who's willing to try.

That's the kind of success I'm going for.

Now it's your turn.

What do you want?

The possibilities are limitless—and, as we'll see in the next chapter, so are you.

As we continue stripping away limiting beliefs and shining a light on the fears lurking in the shadows, your big dreams and desires should be coming more into focus. Let's dive a bit deeper with these journal prompts.

What does entrepreneurship mean to you?

How might you be allowed to be a more authentic version of yourself?

What might entrepreneurship allow you to experience in life?

What might it allow you to achieve?

How might you impact your family and community?

What big dreams would entrepreneurship give you a bridge to?

What desires would come into reach?

CHAPTER 3

LABELS LIMIT GROWTH

We love labels. We have them for our personality types, our experiences, our existing careers, and our comfort levels. Labels can be helpful, and we are going to talk about how we can use them to grow in new and powerful ways. It's when those labels become a box that we can't grow out of that they become a problem.

Don't get me wrong. I know how hard it can be to believe that there's more than the struggle you're in right now, especially for those of us who have spent years not knowing what our purpose might be. This is why our first two chapters focused on possibility instead of logistics. By shifting our perception of entrepreneurship, identifying some hidden mindsets, and starting to dream a little bit, we're building important layers of awareness.

Awareness of what it means to be your own boss in today's actual world, not whatever our old assumptions might be. Awareness of what you truly want, not just what you've been told to want. Awareness of who you *are*, not which label describes you the best.

What I'm about to say doesn't always feel true, because it isn't true 100 percent of the time, but it's important to say anyway: a lot of our limits are self-imposed and based on our perception of ourselves.

Hear me out.

If entrepreneurship is more accessible than you thought, and if your dreams can be bigger than you thought, what if *you're* more than you thought, too?

Spoiler: you definitely are. And I don't mean that in a *do better, get better, be better* kind of way. I mean it in a *you're insanely dynamic* kind of way—in a *you're-never-stuck* kind of way.

I have this belief—based on what I've seen in my life and in the people around me—that what you are meant to do is going to find you eventually. *If* you seek it. The sooner you open yourself up to the possibility that your purpose finds *you*, the less time, energy, and pain you'll have to endure in a life that's not aligned with your truest self.

Because of this belief, I am confident that the work we're doing here—both the literal entrepreneurial work and the internal work it requires—creates a richer, more fulfilling life. One that feels like *yours*.

We have to understand just how dynamic—and changeable—you are in the first place. Together we're facing the sometimes uncomfortable (but actually pretty liberating) truth that nothing is permanent. Not even our personalities.

I'll go first.

My Story: I Go after What I Want

Trying new things to make my life less miserable was a pretty consistent theme in my life throughout my twenties. Sometimes in healthy ways, sometimes not so much. One desperate attempt to change happened when I was working at a little wine-and-cheese shop in college.

First of all, a wine shop is not the place for someone who is not good friends with alcohol. The people I worked with didn't seem to share those realizations, because they were definitely alcoholics who spent the day drinking. This was more or less encouraged by the shop because our rule was that we could *only* have what the store offered as samples while we were on the clock. Anything else, even water, we had to buy. On my broke college budget, buying fancy water was off the table. So was the wine (even though it was offered to me over and over again). That left coffee, chocolate, and cheese. All day long. I know this sounds kind of amazing, but trust me, by the end of a Saturday shift when the owners weren't on-site, I'd be bloated and completely jacked—a full-on eyes-twitching, caffeinated, and sugar-fueled disaster.

Brain and body misery aside, the owners being off-site made Saturdays the best day of the week. Working for people who drank a ton was not on my list of top-ten goals for my twenties. Or ever. Jobs are hard to come by when you live in a tiny town, but my eyes were open. Literally, anything else would have been better.

While I waited for an opportunity to open up, I was still attending school to become [insert one of my ever-changing majors here]. That was also the year I took my favorite class ever—a seminar class that exposed us to different jobs that you could get with science-based degrees: an ecologist who worked to protect the nearby forest I loved so much; a well-known medicinal herb grower and formulator; and a biologist who studied invasive species and created statewide action plans to remedy issues. Finally, a class with real-life examples that felt tangible. And my favorite day inside of my favorite class was the day I met Michael.

It was an on-site day at a paper mill nearby that was listed as one of the top 100 most toxic places in the US. We were there to learn about the cleanup process through a tour of the facility. Michael led a team on the development side of the operation as well as our tour for the day. And he was hilarious. His quintessential New England sarcasm had me cracking up.

After the tour, I approached him and told him I'd like to work for him.

He was just as chill and kind as he'd seemed on the tour, but he told me, "We don't have a job opening right now, thanks."

So I asked for his email, and then I emailed him about hiring me.

There was still no job, he told me. So I asked him to make me a job. The faux confidence here came from the desire to leave my shitty work environment. I had nothing to lose and everything to gain.

I had ideas about what that might look like, but Michael wasn't biting. He ignored all my emails. I wasn't giving up.

And then...

One day...

At my wine-and-cheese-shop job...

I looked up, and there he was—totally unsuspecting—just there to buy a bottle of wine. I basically cornered him while he was shopping. I had an inescapable smile and total confidence that this was my big chance.

"Hi! Remember me?"

He couldn't have been as excited as I was about this seemingly serendipitous moment. He knew what was coming. I asked *yet again* about a job.

"There is *no job*, Sarah. I'm not sure what you want me to do."

But I was sure there was an opportunity here, and I laid out the internship idea once again and promised to do anything they needed if I could just work *there* instead of where I was.

He finally caved.

After that, whenever he got a chance to introduce me, he'd proudly tell people, "This is Sarah, the intern. She basically forced me to create a job for her."

I still consider him a mentor and friend long after working for him. The job he created for me helped shape my path to where I am today. It also shaped my self-perception. I realized I could create opportunities. Seeing an opportunity where there was none, going after it, and getting it became part of my story about who I am.

Initially, what was an out-of-character series of behaviors became part of the way in which I viewed myself. You see, I have the core belief that we can cultivate different parts of ourselves, which came from a very impactful childhood experience. At seven years old, I was in a study at the National Institute of Health for children with ADHD. Here they experimented with how much Ritalin to put me on until they determined 40 mg a day was the right dose for me.

From second grade to sixth grade, I was an excellent student. But when my mom's intuition rightfully kicked in, and she had me taken off this extraordinary amount of stimulants, I suddenly didn't have this powerful tool that was helping me concentrate anymore. And I was a mess. But I distinctly remember thinking, *I know what it feels like to concentrate, and I can practice that.* And so I did. Eventually, I turned my chaotic and high energy into a superpower (now that I know how to work with it).

To this day I wonder if out-of-character moments are truly out of character, or if they're glimpses into who we *really* are. And I definitely believe we can cultivate different aspects of ourselves through practice. These are two beliefs that have served me well on this journey.

Now that you understand a little bit more about how I see myself, you can appreciate how I got myself into a mess early on. It was actually a situation that came to a head just before the trip to Bali—remember how I'd just lost a huge part of my income due to ethical misalignment? Don't worry, it wasn't Michael. But it was a client that I'd pursued in a similar way, and I was so proud that it worked.

This time, the person I wanted to work with had spoken at a conference I attended. Their content was really intriguing, and I was feeling confident in my marketing skills by that point. After the event, I sent off an email that set the wheels in motion. Then follow-ups, pressing forward, getting an in-person interview, holding my ground on working remotely, and eventually landing it. The money was great. The terms of the agreement were great. It checked all of the boxes that you'd want in order to feel stable and secure as a gig worker, which made leaving feel that much worse.

The real problem wasn't that I had to leave. It's that a part of me had known from the in-person interview that I shouldn't have been there at all. Looking back, my intuition had been screaming. After the first full day of the interview process, I went back to my hotel and cried my eyes out for hours.

You know that feeling you get when something is just off, but you can't put your finger on it? It was a terrible sinking feeling in my gut that just got heavier and heavier during my on-site visit and interview. I couldn't make sense of the inner alarm system going off because I hadn't yet cultivated the trust in my intuition that I have today. So I wrote it all off as imposter syndrome and fear. I even beat myself up for being so scared. Which meant I had to ignore all the feels that were coming up. I mean, I'm the person who (*checks notes*) makes shit happen! I see opportunity and go for it! I'm not the person who gets this far and walks away because she's a little overwhelmed.

The thing is, the CEO, who had been so impressive at the conference, was a typical billionaire bropreneur, bragging about how good he was at making his money through others. I ignored that too, and told myself my feelings were because I was intimidated. It was easier to ignore as time went on because I hardly interacted with him on a daily basis. I loved the rest of the team; they were my people—scientists. But then it hit the fan when I got a call from someone on the internal team telling me that the lead scientist quit because of ethical misalignment with the marketing materials. Apparently, I was being spoon-fed half-truths (and sometimes downright lies). I became a medical copywriter, in part, to ensure I was spreading truthful, genuinely helpful content. And I had been seriously duped. I thought I was going to throw up.

He wasn't just bragging about making money. He was proud of how manipulative he could be in doing so. The entire time I was writing for him, I was doing the dirty work of misrepresenting the products and the company to customers and investors. And I had no idea. My nausea and stomach knots suddenly made sense. I was furious at myself.

Since I refused to compromise my ethics for money, I terminated my contract immediately. While the part of me who moved ahead in spite of fear was alive and well, the part of me who listened to her intuition was just starting to find her footing.

Real quick: let's get curious about some of the labels that you have given yourself and how they sometimes show up in your life as a blessing and other times as a curse.

What are some labels that you identify with? Like my "I'm the person who gets shit done." You might be "the perfectionist," "the shy one," "the one who is always responsible," or "the one who never finishes anything." Write a list of any that come to mind.

Now think of a time that this label was a superpower and worked in your favor, supporting what you were trying to accomplish. Write it out.

Next, think of a time when that same label has limited you, got you in trouble, or otherwise created obstacles preventing you from being your best self.

Breaking Out of the Box

There's a lot I *could* unpack from those two stories, but only because I'm writing about them right now. We're not usually working out our deep, dark inner thought processes when we talk to people. Instead, I might explain my get-shit-done persona by just saying, "I'm an Aries, so..." (Actually, Emily would be more likely to say that. She's the keeper of the astrology.) Or I could explain that it was my Enneagram type 2 natural drive to serve that kept me working for that CEO even though he made me queasy. That would segue nicely into an explanation for all of the hours I worked in Bali to make sure no one missed out while I was in a different time zone.

I could refer to my ENFJ preferences, my Myers–Briggs type, my ADHD diagnosis from childhood, my DiSC profile, my Human Design type...and if you resonate with one of those terms, you'd probably understand me better.

I think a key reason people love astrology and personality profiles so much is because it gives us vocabulary that helps us connect to ourselves and each other. For that purpose, labels can be useful. We're complex beings who aren't really taught about our complexity. It makes sense that we'd latch on to personality quizzes and cognitive or emotional frameworks. They help us understand parts of ourselves and communicate that understanding to other people.

The catch is, there's not a single system or theory out there that can be a stand-in for self-awareness or personal development. They can be tools that support you as you grow, but they shouldn't ever stop you from growing. Don't let them be justifications for why you are the way you are, ultimately building yourself a limiting box of labels.

Being a fiery Aries or an earthy Taurus might explain some of your natural inclinations, but it doesn't mean the Aries can't ground or the Taurus can't find a spark. And no one is doomed to fail as an entrepreneur just because they have a certain personality type. If you don't feel like you're naturally equipped with the traits that contribute to success as a business owner, you simply need to cultivate them. Some will come more easily than others.

Personality Isn't Permanent

The number one self-limiting belief that I see holding people back is the idea that who we are is fixed. It's my great pleasure to inform you that...it's not. You are incredibly dynamic. Your brain and even your DNA are far more malleable than we've been led to believe. And your environments, both inside and out, impact you profoundly.

There's a myth floating around that says your brain can't tell the difference between visualization and actually doing something, but that's not exactly true. Dr. Andrew Huberman talked about this recently. He's one of my favorite resources for a scientific approach to personal development because he's both thorough and practical. Neuroscientist and professor at Stanford University School of Medicine, Dr. Huberman teaches that your brain is too smart to be tricked by a visualization, but it does change when you implement a practice. When you imagine that something is true, you create a new neural pathway toward that truth. The more you reinforce it, the stronger it becomes.

That means repeating affirmations, forming new habits, or just imagining something over and over again can change the actual structure of your brain and create less resistance to that change.

You can quite literally hack your brain.

And it's not just your brain that can change—your genetic expression can too. Without getting too far into the weeds, the science of epigenetics refers to a series of chemical tags on your DNA, held in what's called the epigenome. This center controls the way your cells read your genes, and that reading can change. Like a plant will grow in direction and size based on environmental factors, your epigenome can also shift, to some extent, through the seasons of your life. Your environment, stress, habits, and choices all play a part in turning bits of your DNA on or off, up or down, changing how they're expressed. We've allowed the belief that our DNA is some sort of fixed code to keep us small and stagnant for far too long.

In other words, nothing is entirely fixed, not even your genetics. You're not stuck. You're dynamic. And placebo and nocebo results in studies tell us that our beliefs play a powerful role in impacting our biology. If you don't feel like you're the "right" kind of person to be an entrepreneur, or that what you want to create in the world is outside of the box you've always seen yourself in, it's okay. You have so much more potential inside of you than what's already been expressed, and there's no way to know how much change that represents without going for it.

My personality is dynamic. I am full of potential and possibilities. I am in a constant state of creating myself.

Personality Is Contextual

You know how sometimes your response to an invitation from a friend can be *Part of me wants to, and part of me doesn't*? Hold on to that feeling, because it's exactly what you need to understand that we are made up of many internal parts. And when we know we're made up of a system of parts, we can be much more forgiving of our contradictions and mixed emotions.

It's perfectly human to have contradictory feelings, and it's a sign of growth to think differently now than you did in the past. So why do we put so much pressure on ourselves to figure it all out *and stay that way forever*? The fear of looking a certain way or no longer *being* a certain way can be incredibly limiting. We don't want to contradict ourselves. We don't want to look unstable or flighty. We don't want to change, because sometimes that means admitting we were once wrong. And if we were once wrong, who's to say we aren't wrong now?

But if you accept that there are many truths and that different parts of you can have conflicting feelings about a situation, then you can permit yourself to contradict your former self, whether that self is from five minutes or five decades ago. When you embrace the dynamic human you truly are, you prime yourself for even more growth to come.

Time isn't the only factor, either. *Personality is contextual* and this applies to almost every situation. Think about it: you don't always behave the same way around your mom as you would around your romantic partner(s). Does that mean you're being inauthentic around one or the other? Of course not. You can be yourself no matter who you're with—which sides you show may vary based on safety, comfort, and so many other factors.

This is where the study of psychology can give us tools—understanding our desire to appear consistent, as well as the reality that we're multifaceted and complex, frees us up to be ourselves in the fullest way.

I am a multifaceted being, and I celebrate the beauty in my complexities. I release the need to be consistent, and I embrace honest and authentic growth. I give myself permission to unapologetically and fully be my dynamic self.

Personal Growth before Business Growth

A beautiful side effect of allowing yourself to view yourself as parts of a whole rather than a single, constant *you* is that you don't have to overidentify with your emotions or make them who you are. Part of you can be sad or hurt. Part of you can be excited. Part of you can be afraid. All of you can be in the right place even if some part of you doesn't feel comfortable.

How do you bring the different parts of you together in that aligned life we talked about pages ago? With compassionate curiosity. There's almost nothing more damaging to growth than pretending to know everything. This is a pervasive problem in the boomer generation, who tends to think it's a sign of confidence. But when you already *know*, your mind is closed. You are fixed. You are what you are (even if that has six different personality type labels on it). And you have no reason to change.

The antidote to a fixed mindset is curiosity.

When you're curious, you're open to new ideas, concepts, and ways of being. You're genuinely interested in things that encourage growth, including why one part of you wants to hang with your friend and another doesn't. And when you pair that open-mindedness with compassion around whatever you discover—**chef's kiss**.

Compassionate curiosity is your secret weapon for serious growth and healing; personal growth is your secret weapon for business growth and healing your relationship to work, money, and success itself. Put them together, and it's how you can create a life far beyond the dreams you have today.

There is someone out there who is less qualified than I am, less experienced than I am, and less prepared than I am, doing what I want to do and thriving; I have the right to thrive as well.

The Identity Gap

It wasn't until I started doing this work that I realized so much of the anger, frustration, pain, depression, and anxiety I was experiencing in life was directly related to how much of my authentic self I was trying to bury. I've always been an intuitive person, but I haven't always listened to that intuition or accepted it as part of my identity. In fact, I lost myself completely for a while. I would get pulled around by what other people told me was right for me or by what I thought I was supposed to think, say, or do. But what they were telling me was rarely what I knew about myself or what I needed. I only listened to them because of fear.

Case in point: lots of people told me not to put any pole-dancing content on my Instagram. It's one of my passions and a huge part of how I spend my time. I'm proud of the work that goes into it and the results that come out. Why wouldn't I share something that important to me?

Just because it still had a little bit of stigma around it?

Sorry, not sorry—I became an entrepreneur in part so I didn't have to hide parts of myself in order to fit other people's definition of professional.

That doesn't mean I felt *great* about it. I still had butterflies when I hit publish on those posts and still worried a little bit about how people would respond.

But when I looked at those feelings, they weren't my intuition telling me it was a bad idea to share that part of myself online. They were feelings of fear, which the people telling me not to post were probably feeling too.

The difference is subtle.

Fear is trying to keep you in safe, understandable boxes. Intuition is trying to lead you closer to alignment with your own values—with who you really are.

When I say that you can cultivate aspects of your personality, I mean *your own, true self,* not characteristics you've been told are virtuous or successful or worthy. If you attempt to cultivate elements that are not true to you but believe you *should* be cultivating, you'll experience frustration and resistance. I'm sure you have something in your life right now that causes you immense frustration. Ask yourself—is the frustration telling you that thing is out of alignment with your core values?

The goal is to get really clear about who you are, without judgment, even though we live in a world that values consistency and does judge the shit out of us. The more you look like and fit into the world around you, especially as you were growing up, the harder this is going to be. All the kids who grew up LGBTQIA+ and on the margins got a head start on personal growth because they had to define themselves—there was no box for them to fit in. As a bi woman, I see how this part of me fueled my quest for self-acceptance and understanding. I'm so deeply grateful for the humans in this world whose identities don't fit in boxes because they are on the frontier of change. They are making it easier for everyone else to be authentically themselves even if they don't identify as queer. Pushing back on societal expectations when necessary allows you to find and embrace the unique life you were meant to lead.

Unfortunately, our amazing, changeable brains are also fear-predicting machines. Without intentional effort in the opposite direction, they will usually default to stress and fear and the responses that stress and fear generate.

Looking back on that experience with the client I walked away from, it's clear that I knew I wasn't supposed to be there *and* that I didn't know how to say so. To myself or anyone else. At the time, I barely even noticed that the other woman who was there had quit before the interview process was over. She knew. And she listened to herself a little better than I did.

I interpreted my emotions as fear and imposter syndrome during the interviews, and I believed fear was supposed to be ignored. I didn't get curious. I stuffed those feelings down deep and even called myself weak. I had set out, my labels leading the way, to get shit done. I didn't stop to wonder what nuggets of truth and wisdom my intuition had for me. I didn't get curious about the parts of me that were raising the alarm, even though my whole body was amplifying the warning.

Later, when it was clear I needed to quit, I was definitely feeling fear. Walking away from something that feels secure is not easy. I ignored the fear in that situation too, but something was different about it. This fear was showing up because I knew I had to do something brave in order to maintain my integrity. Unlike my fear at the initial interview, which was warning me I was walking into something massively out of alignment with my values.

One of the most important practices I have implemented in my life came directly from this devastating situation. That is, learning to intentionally differentiate between fear and intuition. Physically, they can feel really similar—for me it means an elevated heart rate, shallow breathing, butterflies, flushing red, and a welling of mixed and confusing emotions.

When I start to feel those signals, I know it's time to check in with myself and try to name what's behind them.

So how do you tell the difference between fear that's keeping you small and intuition that's pushing you into sometimes-scary spaces? I wish I had clear, easy answers for you. But remember, this isn't about what works for me—it's about you stepping into your own growing, changing, beautiful personality and creating your ideal life from there. I can give you some things to practice, but you'll have to get curious and learn through that practice what intuition and authenticity look like for you.

I notice more readily things that are out of alignment with who I am and how I want to show up. I tap into courage to take steps to close this identity gap.

Develop Your Intuition

Even with all of the recent advances in science and technology, there is so much we still don't know about the human brain and body. Recent discoveries in epigenetics, gut microbiota, and the glymphatic and endocannabinoid systems are examples of how little we really know about what makes us humans. Research is still ongoing and is very recent in the grand timeline of history, even though these components have been a part of the human experience all along.

I'm saying this now so that you'll be more open to what I'm about to say next, regardless of your relationship to spirituality and the more meta aspects of life. Not having scientific explanations for certain aspects of the human body and brain (yet) doesn't mean we should disregard their existence. The deeper I got into science, the more I realized how little we know. If we don't actively acknowledge this, leaving space for the unknown, we create bigger blind spots for ourselves.

So, whether or not we know how it works, we do know that intuition is real, probably as a subset of the subconscious. The subconscious is taking in way more information than what we can consciously be aware of—something like 94 percent of our brain function—and if intuition helps us tap into that wealth of knowledge, it can be worth listening to.

For the record, this used to be a "fixed" part of my personality. I was the science kid, not the intuitive. That identity stayed top of mind for years and definitely kept me disconnected from the deeper, more authentic parts of myself. But that doesn't mean my intuition was turned off. It just showed up in really inconvenient ways, like unexplained crying and a knot in my stomach.

Your experience of your intuition will be different, and you can only learn where to find it by making a practice of looking for it.

If you suddenly do something on impulse that takes you out of your comfort zone—and you have no idea why—ask yourself questions. Think about what set your feet in motion. See if you can identify what that impulse is telling you about who you are and what you want. Instead of assuming it was "out of character," ask if maybe it was your buried authentic self peeking her head out temporarily to make herself known.

If your body is behaving strangely or something feels "off," try to turn some compassionate curiosity inward to see if something's up. If you're getting a weird feeling about something and don't know if it's fear or intuition, try asking yourself questions. I'll share some of my favorite questions shortly. But the point is to spend time consciously thinking about the subconscious and see what you find out.

Think about the subconscious mind and beliefs as a cave of shadows, and curiosity is a flashlight. The shadows look scary enough at first glance that most people spend their lives avoiding them. But when equipped with the flashlight of curiosity, you can bring these old stories and beliefs into the light, and when they're in the light, they can grow and transform.

Getting to know yourself (maybe for the first time ever) is not an easy task. There aren't right and wrong answers, and you won't always succeed. Sometimes the only way to know that a decision isn't a good fit for you is to make the decision and realize it's wrong.

As you set out to learn more about yourself, here are some things you might watch out for. When they come up, remember to be compassionately curious—the world might tell you to suppress or judge them, but I think they're great indicators of who you are underneath all the societal conditioning and limiting beliefs.

Triggery emotions. Jealousy and judgment especially. These feelings tell us more about us than about the people we direct them toward. Case in point: bropreneurs are an easy target for our judgment not just because the caricature is obnoxious, but because deep down we know that we could *and should* be just as successful as they are. So why aren't we? And what success is it that we're craving?

"Out of character" choices—like when I demanded a job that first time. I had always been a hard worker and had wanted to be financially independent since I was a kid. But I hadn't gone after a job quite like that before I started bugging

Michael to create a role for me. It felt like a confident piece of me took center stage, and I let it happen. After that, it became part of how I saw my personality.

Nagging feelings. Specifically, recurring feelings of frustration, desire, or longing. A job that you want to quit, a gig you should pass on, a slime project you want to make with your daughters, a degree you want to drop out of, a course you want to take, a service you want to offer. Those are all clues pointing to something true about yourself. Even picking up this book in the first place is a clue that part of you wants to create something new in your life.

Whenever your intuition speaks up—however it speaks up—be as kind to it as you would be to a friend. Listen. Get to know it (you). See your potential. Create the opportunity. You're free to create a life of your own imagining *as long as you allow your truest self to imagine.*

My compassionate curiosity illuminates the fears, limiting beliefs, and old stories that keep me small. I trust that by examining the clues within my triggery emotions, out-of-character choices, and nagging feelings, I am actively creating a stronger, wiser, more resilient me.

Be Your Own Boss...and Mentor, Coach, and Friend

Recognizing and listening to your intuition is a skill that takes practice. If this doesn't come naturally to you, that's okay. It didn't for me either. It took Emily asking me questions like

"Is this fear or intuition talking?" and "Does this make you feel big or small?" to help distinguish between intuition that's leading me toward expansive experiences and fear that's trying to keep me small because it feels "safe." Each time I stretched my intuitive muscles and tried to get closer to my own hopes and dreams, I laid down new neural pathways that made it easier and easier to do it all again.

Stretching those muscles can be challenging and confusing because discomfort has its place and isn't always meant to be pushed through. There *are* times when discomfort comes from leaving your comfort zone even though you know you need to. But sometimes discomfort is your body giving you a warning that your conscious mind isn't recognizing, and that's something you should listen to.

In those cases, ask yourself the second question from a moment ago: play out the likely result of an action and ask yourself, "Does this make me feel big or small?"

When you imagine yourself as a successful entrepreneur, what are the dominant feelings that come with that image? Do you feel proud and empowered at the idea of being your own boss, even if the responsibility scares you? How does it make you feel about your agency?

If something is causing you emotional turmoil, try to imagine what life will look like on the other side of that turmoil. Would going through it be worth it? Would you be proud of yourself and what you accomplished? If so, your distress is probably coming from fear. If you're still full of questions and unsure if it's worth it, think about what feelings you're associating with it.

Confusion and anxiety are normal when stepping out of your comfort zone. But if it goes beyond that to things like shame, guilt, hopelessness, or disempowerment, there's something more to pay attention to.

Throughout this chapter, you might have noticed positive statements where other chapters have had exercises for you to do or questions for you to answer. If you aren't familiar with affirmations, they are simply statements of what's true (or what will be true) and are a seriously powerful way to literally change your mind.

Now that we've spent some time thinking about how limitless you really are, give some affirmations of your own a try.

I am...
I have...
I can...
I will...

CHAPTER 4

MICROBETS WIN THE GAME

The only book I've ever read twice is *The Slight Edge*, by Jeff Olson. I don't remember who first recommended it to me or where I picked it up. It was around the time I was in rehab. At that time, I was hungry for anything that could help me turn my life around. You know how it goes—we collect all sorts of books, advice, and ideas without really thinking twice about it. Most of them wind up collecting dust. Some of them change your life. This book was one of those change-your-life moments, and I had no idea it was coming.

Because I was in my "make life suck less" era, any changes I made were going to have to be small and incremental—tiny, even. And that's what *The Slight Edge* is about—making small habits and adjustments in your life and trusting that the compounding power of these tiny actions will lead to big changes.

The book taught me how to set intentions, how to take first steps, and how to keep calibrating along the way. Those small steps start long journeys. Small adjustments make big changes. I joke that it's done more to reduce my anxiety than any form of therapy I've tried. It's not really much of a joke, either—my anxiety levels are significantly lower thanks to the idea that microactions have a profound impact on my quality of life.

While I used the principles in *The Slight Edge* daily and would talk about the book to anyone who would listen, I didn't actually pick it up again until years later, when registrations started to come in for my course. I got so excited about the futures of everyone trusting me to support them and was so grateful to all of the people who joined that I wanted to send them a gift. *The Slight Edge* immediately came to mind.

Since I couldn't just send people a book I hadn't read in five-plus years, I picked it up again just to skim it and make sure it was as good as I remembered...and before I knew it, I was reading the whole damn thing over again. It was just as good, if not better. I broke out the highlighter and everything.

Since that first class of hopeful souls joined my program, I've continued to refer to *The Slight Edge* and recommend it to my students. Today, language from that book has permeated our writing community—setting intentions and course correcting all make sense to us. If you haven't read the book, those terms refer to the importance of saying what we want out loud and defining goals even when we don't know how to reach them, looking for what we need to get there, and making changes along the way.

I won't tell you all of the stories or examples (seriously, you just need to read the book), but there's one you should know about because it's such a powerful and helpful image. It's attached to course correcting. Jeff is teaching us to prepare to make lots of small adjustments over time, and he tells the story of the mission to the moon. This is perfect because so many of our big goals feel like "moon shots"—so big and so far away that it's hard to know how we'll ever get there. Apparently, from the time that particular Apollo mission took off to the time it landed with the first humans to step foot on the moon, the rocketship was off course 97 percent of the time.

Ninety. Seven. Percent.

That's not even trying for perfection. That's focusing on a constant effort to get back on track. And they made it to the fucking *moon* that way!

Simple actions compound over time.

All you need are minor course corrections when you realize you've veered off in the "wrong" direction. They're not the most dramatic moves, but small steps have exponential power to take you where you want to go, *even if you don't know exactly where that is yet.* After all, when I read *The Slight Edge* for the first time, I was an event planner working to be a better freelance writer, and I thought online courses were *so cliché*.

This is what achieving a giant goal actually looks like. It's what we do as entrepreneurs every day. Not something big and grand that happens all at once if only we'd get it just right, but something we can adjust, incrementally, over and over again until we finally reach the moon.

The Unsexy Secret to Success

Before mundane movie characters transform into their heroic selves, what has to happen first? Usually, months of training, conditioning, and eating healthy. The film industry, desperate to make this essential but boring process entertaining, clips it all together and condenses it into a one- to three-minute montage set to fast-paced, exciting music. And because even that's not enough, they throw in other elements to spice things up—their kid sitting on their back while they do push-ups, them punching meat hanging in a cooler, them overtaking their trainer, or them acclimating to cold temps by sitting in an ice cream truck. ("Sanka, ya dead mon?")

No one is interested in watching someone slowly learn a new skill.

Living it out sucks even more.

In our own lives, we don't skip microsteps because they're hard or inaccessible. We skip them because they're boring. And because we don't realize their power.

The answer to business growth can't possibly be personal growth, can it? I'm not improving my chances as an entrepreneur by bringing more balance into my life, am I? Yeah, yeah, journaling, affirmations, whatever. Tell me how I can launch something cool, or quit my shitty job, or, or, or...

Get me to the good stuff.

But the real secret to success is to give the unsexy stuff the meaning it deserves. If you want to have a different experience in this world, focus on what's in front of you. Trust that every little change you make and every practice you establish is bringing you closer to that experience you've envisioned.

And if you can't quite trust that yet, at least try to stop beating yourself up about not being where you want to be. Remember: even after the big training montage and epic fight, Rocky still didn't win.

Judging your journey by how close you are (or aren't) to some epic victory is not helping you get to that victory. I have been there; my students have been there; I'm willing to *bet* (ha) that you've been there too. For me, the stakes were high. The days where I beat myself up were the days I would drink. Maybe you can relate, maybe not. Either way, that shit doesn't get you anywhere. So take the steps you can take, and until you can trust yourself and the future you're building, trust me when I tell you that you're doing enough.

Taking care of yourself and making slow progress might not make the final film cut, but the confidence, power, and amazing future you're building? That's sexy AF.

Montage Moments

Remember when we talked about letting go of the need to get college degrees before you can start over? That's a great example of something big and dramatic that might feel like the right choice with a tangible outcome. It's not necessarily the unsexy montage moment that feels like a given or (worse) like a waste of time. The old gatekeepers are distractions. Everything you need is out there, in small doses that you can add a little at a time. Here are some examples:

- Take an online course.
- Fall down the rabbit hole on something that interests you every Friday evening.
- Remove something that doesn't help. (For me? Alcohol.)
- Add something good. Like a salad or a morning walk.
- Go after clients you don't feel ready for.
- Find a mentor.
- Learn a new skill from a mentor.

- Constantly remind yourself that everyone started at the beginning.
- Create a morning routine.
- Challenge your fears with affirmations.
- Question your core beliefs about yourself and the world.
- Make small promises to yourself and keep them.
- (Add yours!)

Make the Most of the Compound Effect

Small, everyday choices may seem like nothing at the time, but they're actually moving us toward an entirely different future. And isn't that such a relief? Knowing that you don't need to take grandiose action to see profound results?

This book (or any personal development book) is a good example of a microdecision that could have serious compounding effects in the future.

Buying this book, or borrowing it from a friend, didn't really commit you to anything. You're not investing a ton of money. You're just spending a few hours exploring a new way of thinking. Easy. Maybe too easy. Maybe easy enough that you're wondering how much good it'll actually do.

But here's where the compound effect kicks in: this probably isn't the first time you've read something about entrepreneurship. Maybe you've read books. Maybe you've invested in classes and training. Or maybe you've just seen some blog posts or heard someone talking about it. Something opened you up to the possibility of working for yourself, and that something-else is swirling around in your mind as you read.

Those previous small moments—other books, blogs, classes, conversations—didn't just dissipate when they ended. Everything you're reading now is affected (compounded) by them. If I say something that contradicts what you've heard before, you have the opportunity to decide what's true for you and the path you're on. If I say something that echoes what you've heard before, that idea may get a little more cemented in your mind. Marketers say that it takes a lot of repeated exposure to an idea before you will trust it, so every time you consume content like this, you're increasing your exposure and getting a little closer to acceptance. The simple action (reading, listening) compounds.

This goes for literally everything. Reading. Watching YouTube videos about a skill you're interested in. Hanging out with another local entrepreneur once a week. Making your morning coffee in that one way that is familiar and delicious and makes you smile. Going for walks. Saying *no* more often. Saying *yes* when it's a hell yes.

Small, simple actions compound and result in big changes over time.

I don't know how this concept is landing for you, but when I first read Jeff's book, I latched on to it immediately. At that time, I needed that injection of hope, and I'm still energized by it today. When I can't manage to make huge changes all at once, knowing that whatever I *can* do will eventually pay off helps me sleep better at night. That's good news for someone with very little bandwidth and a very big desire for life to feel better.

Raise Your Baselines

We're talking about the path to success, but what if you don't even know what "success" means? Or what an ideal path toward it might look like? Congrats—you're totally and completely normal.

The passion track always intimidated me. I had too many interests and not one thing that kept my attention for long. It felt like I had to have too much figured out, or that I had to make a major commitment before I could get started. And that felt too risky.

The good news is when you decide to make good (small) decisions each day, knowing that you'll have to course correct along the way, the exact direction doesn't matter. You can shape your path before taking steps, or you can take steps without knowing exactly what path you're on because success is just reaching a new level. You can do that incrementally, across different areas of life and your business, whether or not you know where you want to be in the future.

I call this raising your baselines, but before you can do this, you have to know what level your starting point is.

If this is the first time you've considered these levels, it can feel a bit overwhelming to see that you aren't where you want to be, probably in many (or all) of the categories. Try to just take note for now, with as little judgment as possible.

On a scale of 1 to 10, with 1 being the least satisfied and 10 being the most satisfied, note how you feel about these areas of your life:

Relationships

- List the five people you interact with most.
- How loved and appreciated do you feel by each?
- How fully can you be yourself with them?
- How connected do you feel to them?
- How satisfied are you with your communication with each?

Connection

- How often do you connect with other people?
- Are you part of any meaningful online communities?
- Do you have any in-person social groups you are a part of?
- What is your relationship with nature like?

Health

- How do you feel about your overall health?
- How is your relationship to exercise (whatever that looks like for you and your ability levels)?
- How well do you prioritize your own health?
- Do you have time to do the type of physical activity you enjoy most?

Money

- How do you feel about what you earn?
- When you think of money, do you feel calm?
- How do you feel about your savings?
- With struggle on one end of the spectrum and empowerment on the other, where do you fall in your relationship with money?

Career

- How do you feel when someone asks you about what you do for work?
- Do you feel like your work matters?
- How do you feel about the people you work with?
- When you look ahead, are you inspired by the possibilities of your career?

Fulfillment

- Do you often do things that light you up and energize you?
- Do you feel like you get to experience a state of flow on a regular basis?
- How often do you feel like you push yourself into something new?
- How often do you engage in activities that strengthen your creativity?

Now that you're looking at your baselines, what feels like your most pressing need? Not just the lowest baseline, but the lowest one that you can move with the least amount of effort. Or more importantly, what baseline would impact the rest if you could raise it?

Take some time here to really look at each area to decide what to work on first. If you can't decide, I'll give you a hint: for most of us, especially once we've started to build our businesses, *connection* is the place to start. (Though health is also often a top contender.)

You'll notice I separated connection from relationships. That's because there's more to connection than your relationships with close friends and family. Connection is a key part of that area of life, and in a post-pandemic world, many of us are basically starved for it.

When I mentor entrepreneurs one-on-one, I often tell them to work *less* while they're trying to achieve their next layer of growth. That was the case for an amazing woman named Amanda—and honestly, neither one of us expected just how much that one baseline had been pulling everything else down.

She had been living on her parents' couch; she found my program, and it helped get her out into her own apartment. Her writing was great already. She just needed some help with her business. When we looked at her business to identify what would help her level up, I saw immediately she needed to build more connection in her life. The apartment was empty. She had no roommates. Her dog had just passed away. And the pandemic had sealed her in. Working all day to earn more money but never leaving the house was making her miserable, and her misery was starting to show up in her interactions with clients. The most important thing her business needed was for her to be a whole person apart from it.

She joined Bumble BFF, nervous and awkward but willing to give it a shot. The timing was actually great—everyone was coming out of the pandemic, and we were all a bit awkward reentering society. She and I talked about leaning into that dynamic and connecting over how disconnected we all are, and it worked! Soon, she started dating. She fostered a dog. Her life started to take shape apart from work. She was happier. Calmer. More connected.

What happened next? She started getting clients. When those clients came in, she took the same unapologetic tact as she had on her Bumble BFF intros: she stopped beating herself up for where she could have been and started leaning in on where she was. Rather than adding a bunch of new services, she doubled down on what worked.

It's counterintuitive to think we should do less to make more, but studies say we're only productive for about six hours anyway. Attention spans aren't made to sit down and crank out workdays much longer than that. I like to try for six hours when I'm not actively growing something. After that, or any time trying isn't getting me anywhere, I shift. Another baseline can always use my attention.

All too often, freelancers and business owners build businesses that run them rather than the other way around. Being hyperfocused on building the business, making more money, or getting more clients creates a sense of scarcity. And that scarcity pulls focus from the whole human with a whole life who's working on those problems in the first place. I often recommend to students to work fewer hours and make space for something that brings them joy in the afternoon. If you can't imagine shortening your workday, you may have too much on your plate or too many expectations for how to manage everything. Time to course correct, in that case—you've got some baselines to raise!

I often refer to Future Sarah as a separate person from myself when I don't want to do something in the moment–doing the dishes, for example. I'll often say to myself, *Future Sarah will be grateful that I've done the dishes and cleaned the house so that when I get up in the morning, I can jump right into my morning routine.*

I always assume Future Sarah is a more capable version of myself, which makes it easier for me to make choices in alignment with a better me–rather than being held back by current baselines. I make decisions to help Future Sarah because I know she's going to be better at her decision-making if the things I can control now are taken care of.

Future Sarah is an intention that I can set in the present and trust we'll find our way there.

You're consistently cultivating a new, more competent version of yourself, and you can't predict where you'll be three months, six months, or a year from now. If you do this work, the version of you in that future is not the same version of you that is reading this book today. But if you *could* imagine Future You, what might that person be capable of?

Spend some time here dreaming about how badass you're becoming, and what kinds of things you're thinking about now that could be handed off to that much more experienced You.

Here are a few prompts to get the creative juices flowing:

What are three decisions that you are not truly able to make just yet that you can pass off to Future You?

What are three worries that you can't solve right now that you can trust capable Future You with?

What are three small things (that take fifteen minutes or less) that you can do today as a gift to Future You?

Now, let's write a couple of affirmations:

I trust Future Me to...

I support Future Me by...

Nothing Is Wasted

My first self-employed venture was an event planning service. I've told you this already. What I haven't told you is how much I hated it. Not just at the time, either. I hated it so much that for a while I couldn't even talk about it. I didn't even want to think about it. *Cross that whole stage of life off, please.* Though I knew better, to some extent, it took a long time to see how an event planning business could benefit the business I have now. It had been a complete waste of time, I was sure of it.

Then, in 2019, when I hosted my first in-person event, I suddenly realized it had all come full circle. In fact, it took someone else telling me, "I love that you do events! I've always been scared to do them" to realize how much good had come from that stage of life. Planning my event had been a breeze—a delight, even. It was SO much more fun to plan an event when I had full say over the end product than when I'd been doing it for clients. There was no one to run things by, no one whose permission I needed to ask. And being scared to invite my students to an in-person event hadn't crossed my mind. I just thought it would be fun, and then I did it. When that person asked me how I learned to put something like that together, I answered without thinking, "It's because I spent three years doing other people's events professionally."

The skills I learned running complicated events for hundreds of people meant I could put together a gathering for seventy students fairly easily. But instead of acknowledging what I'd gained from that detour, I beat myself up for the years wasted going down the wrong path.

When I say "nothing is wasted," I mean *every single thing* you do or have done in life has helped you learn or grow in some way. And ultimately, it's leading you to the path you were always meant to be on.

Maybe you don't feel like you were getting anywhere at that one job or with that business you moved on from—but what if you could change the narrative surrounding that time in your life? Can you see where you learned skills or grew as a person in a way that helps you out now?

Each microdecision in front of you now has a compounding effect—and so did each microdecision Past You made. And it's a bummer, but that momentum is often invisible. The beginning of a compound curve is subtle, so it can seem impossible to feel the growth when we're in it. We kind of have to trust that something good is happening and keep going until we see how it pans out. Staying consistent until we have enough evidence gathered is critical. So many people give up or course correct too early in those beginning stages. It can definitely feel scary to bet on yourself when it's hard to see the growth, but trust me when I say that you're giving yourself a gift by showing up with patience and consistency. Once you have enough evidence gathered to determine the direction you're headed, you can evaluate what works and what doesn't, and therefore make informed decisions on where to maintain the course and where to correct it.

You can't easily see the ROI of a morning routine on your bottom line, and the same thing is true for where you've been.

The thing is, when you're an entrepreneur, personal growth is business growth and vice versa. And most of the time, the growth is hard to measure, but it does not, by any means, make it less valuable.

There's no point in beating yourself up for not being where you want to be in the future, for not doing what you want to do right now, or for taking a path you wish you hadn't on your way here. Take a closer look at all those little choices, mistakes, and wins, and give yourself some credit. You're on a growth journey here.

Where you are—who you are—now is not the same as five or ten years ago. Whether you made a deliberate choice to get here or can't believe how far you've come without realizing it was happening, take a second to celebrate. Feel some gratitude for Past You and everything that person tried and learned and lived through for Present You. Trust that you're going to get to Future You, even if you're not sure how yet.

And get this: not only does every bit of personal and professional growth "count" when you're an entrepreneur, but that growth is also *completely limitless*. This means your business growth is limitless too. Every time you show up for yourself in some way, you benefit, and so does your business. You're not capped by whatever your nine-to-five hands down to you. The momentum may be invisible for a while, but eventually, you'll look back and see where you gathered speed, when you started to streamline a bit, and when the scale finally tipped.

Let yourself show up as the you who planned events, worked in wine-and-cheese shops, and grew your business from rehab. Nothing is wasted. You've gotten yourself this far, and that's worth celebrating.

Embrace Course Corrections

We often choose paths because of our alignment with society, our parents, or simply because of older ideals that we once held. But you can (and should) choose other paths and adjust your steps along the way.

- Look back on your paths to this point and ask where your past choices even came from. Were they your desires or someone else's?
- Identify your values as they are now. When was the last time *you* identified what you want in *your* life?
- Start to explore (just explore!) possible ways to achieve those values.

Compounding Faith

I walked into rehab utterly destroyed.

My self-worth had dropped so low that I no longer wanted to exist. If I could have found a way to completely disappear without hurting my family, I would have done it. My self-loathing had grown so big that I could no longer stand to be around myself. My disconnection with my authentic self had gotten so bad that I couldn't stop drinking on my own. I had become fully convinced that if I continued my drinking as is, I was going to die. Most likely by suicide. Possibly by some unforeseen accident. So I reached out for help and checked myself into rehab.

This wasn't my first time in rehab, but it was the first time I was truly convinced alcohol had no place in my life. Up to that point, I had tried literally everything to keep alcohol in my life in a way that wouldn't hurt me. I finally believed it had to go if I wanted to live.

I also believed I needed to start taking steps that Future Sarah would take. This included waking up and walking down to the ocean every day to watch the sunrise. It included journaling about my gratitude and writing and reading affirmations.

I had to actively, directly combat the overwhelming fears and insecurities I had let build up in my life when I wasn't taking care of myself. One day, after my morning routine was over, I sat down at the kitchen table and cold-emailed prospective clients.

I had been writing for a few years, but when I was drinking, I could barely get client work done. I was relying heavily on content mills, tech-writing gigs, and other odd jobs to scrape together an income. With this chosen sobriety, I decided to start building a base of high-quality clients who would contribute to raising those baselines.

To be clear, this was an extremely painful experience. I was simultaneously growing far outside my comfort zone and trying to heal and repair all the internal damage I had done. My self-loathing was still at an all-time high, even as I reached out to new clients. The only thing motivating me to grow my business was disgust with myself and a desire to live a different life. I don't recommend allowing yourself to get to a point where you can't stand yourself anymore. But for me, a complete spiritual breakdown was necessary before I could start rebuilding. And I began rebuilding—on all fronts—long before I felt ready to do so. I didn't even feel worthy of any of that effort, but a tiny piece of me believed that if I took action before I believed I was worthy, I'd one day believe it.

Today, Sarah Turner Agency is a multimillion-dollar business that helps people break into the world of entrepreneurship. I am so humbled and honored to be part of these beautiful stories. But I didn't know where the hell I was going when I started. My business exists because I did the work before I felt ready or like I deserved any of it, and I might not have kept going if I knew how big it could get. It would have felt too daunting. I simply kept my head down, putting one foot in front of the other, and held a glimmer of hope that Future Sarah would get me the rest of the way there.

Maybe belief and faith are muscles you're still building too. I won't ask you to believe anything blindly, because I don't really know how to pinpoint why I believed *The Slight Edge* when I did or what made that time in rehab my *last* time in rehab. All I know is you've just gotta keep going.

Have you ever had that experience? Where someone tells you how they got something, and you don't wrestle with it at all—you just believe them and adopt it? It's hard to know what makes those particular moments stick. Instead, I am going to ask you to never give up on yourself and to always remain curious. Keep a look out for those inexplicable things that just resonate, and trust that feeling.

I hate personal development books that tell you what to do and then just say, "It'll work," period. I especially hate when the author thinks their way is the only or best way. So if this is your *Slight Edge* moment, that's amazing. Start making small choices meaningful. Start prioritizing personal growth as a means for business growth. Give yourself credit for every ounce of personal development and learning you're able to do, because it's all building invisible momentum, and one day you'll see the exponential growth. And the more you can lean into the business-owner mindset of being an entrepreneur, the more time, energy, and space you'll be able to create for even more growth.

In the meantime, take what works and leave the rest. Start experimenting with the mindsets and actions that work for you. Slow, unsexy trial and error is more than enough.

Let's refer back to the baseline check-in that we did at the beginning of this chapter. It's important to have a starting point—it clarifies which areas need improvement but also provides a marker to see how far you've come.

Cultivating a habit of checking in on your baselines will help you determine if your steps are working. If you're not checking in with yourself and your progress, it's easy to think you're not getting anywhere.

Over time, you'll see things that felt difficult are now easy, stuff that used to scare the shit out of you is not so scary anymore, and things that once felt impossible are now actually happening in your life.

Which sections did you have the lowest scores on?

List the reasons why you believe you scored so low for each separate section.

Refer to the above list; how many of these things are in your direct control to improve upon? Go ahead and circle them.

Write down small, easy-to-do steps (think habits, routines, microdecisions, and simple actions) that you can take to start increasing that score.

Now write down some bigger ideas to raise your baselines that might take some planning and implementing.

What is one thing that you can do today to take action on raising your baselines?

CHAPTER 5

YOU CALL THE SHOTS

I'm always a bit surprised when people say they can't become an entrepreneur because of how time-consuming it is, when I literally decided to start my own business *because* I didn't want to work a forty-hour week. I don't think I'm alone in that, either. Ditching the hours of a nine-to-five is half the appeal. But something about that word "entrepreneur" calls up images of working around the clock to get a business off the ground, neglecting your family to do so, and pouring every spare second into your work just to make sure your business doesn't fail.

The catch is that there are smart ways to build businesses, and then there are not-so-smart ways to build businesses. When people share with me that they have a friend who tried building a business or freelancing but quit because it took up so much time and created so much stress that they were relieved when they went back to a nine-to-five, I usually think to myself, *Wow, I wish they had someone to show them how they could have done that better*. Because I'm willing to bet that person was missing pieces of the puzzle.

It takes a strong skill set, firm boundaries, and constant pushback on limiting beliefs to build a work life that fits around your real life. You quite literally have to design your work to be exactly how you want. And that requires checking in with yourself regularly (and being honest when you do).

I'm gonna go ahead and blame old-school entrepreneurs and the bropreneurs for the misconception. Again. Or in this case, we can call it something like *hustlepreneurship*—because anyone can get caught up in the runaway train of business building, especially when you love the work you're doing. I know I have. I had a whole season of my life where anytime a friend or family member asked me how I was doing, I just replied, "Busy." I had totally bought into the idea that to justify the work I was doing, to make it seem "worthy," I had to hustle and let everyone know just how busy I was.

But you get to decide what you want your business to look like *and* how you want to get there.

That one statement is so loaded with mindset pitfalls that it'll take two chapters to unpack. First, we have to get to the bottom of our relationship with time and the way we think we have to (or can...or can't) use it. Then, in the next chapter, we'll get into our relationship with money itself.

By the end of them both, we'll see that "earning a lot requires working a lot" is as outdated as the idea that you have to open a brick-and-mortar location to be a legit business owner. The entrepreneurial hustle is just not what it used to be—and that's a *really* good thing.

That Anti-Hustle Life

Working nonstop is unnecessary at best and, like we talked about in previous chapters, can actually get in the way of business growth. Rest and reflection are essential elements to growing smarter, not harder. Easier said than believed, though.

Take a student of mine named Amy, for example. She now runs a business that makes more than her nine-to-five while working a fraction of the hours. But before she got to where she is now, she didn't think she had enough time to even take my course, much less build a business. And it's easy to see why. After grinding through a full day of work sandwhiched by ninety minute commutes, then coming home to cook, she was sitting down for dinner with her son at 9:00 every night, just before falling into bed and starting the day all over again. She felt like she was missing out on his life.

Amy's worries aren't unique to her. I've had the same conversation with plenty of other new students. When you're in a place of desperation, adding one more thing to your plate can seem impossible. And as a single mom, Amy couldn't imagine losing any more of what little time she had with her son.

Where was she going to find the time or energy to learn a new skill? Would she have to pour everything she had into building a business, just to eventually make enough money to survive?

This is where hustle culture gets us. That all-or-nothing mentality (that has been romanticized into oblivion) tells us we have to give everything we have and beyond or we don't want it badly enough. You don't have to look far to find someone in the entrepreneur world telling you what else you have to do and who else you have to be like to achieve success. The biggest bullshit message of all is that you should *just do it*, get off your ass, suck it up, and you'll be successful. A message that makes too many people feel discouraged and therefore disregard the idea of entrepreneurship before they even give it a try.

Don't get me wrong. I respond well to tough love, but suggesting it's that simple misses the point. Without even realizing what's happening, you can start working too much, collecting needless certifications, and living by someone else's expectations. But your journey is uniquely yours, and it's not going to look like anyone else's. The idea of building your business from your parents' basement, eating nothing but Ramen, not sleeping, and totally bootstrapping something until it suddenly makes you millions is just. not. necessary.

We didn't dream hustle culture out of thin air. Our whole society is infused with it. We've been programmed since we were children to be cogs in a machine. To believe our worth is tied to our productivity—that suffering somehow proves that we're virtuous and validated. A near impossible standard of all work and delayed play. And so we spin our wheels, barely making ends meet, in a perpetual state of exhaustion and self-deprecation.

The truth is, the life we want is way easier to access than anyone tells us it is. And I don't mean that in a sleazy get-rich-quick way. I mean that even if you wanted to (and could) jump right into total focus on your business, all day every day, with no reason to start slowly with a side hustle, *eighty-hour weeks wouldn't get you any closer to success* than working a few focused hours at a time.

When I tell people to cut back their hours, they're shocked. "But I'm trying to grow my business!" Then I explain how hustle culture works against them and how rest and reflection are essential to growth. Want to know what one of the most rewarding things in the entire world is to me? When they come back absolutely stunned and amazed that the growth is happening while they're working less and taking more time to enjoy their life. We've been sold an idea that suffering and grueling work are virtuous. But I've seen time and time again how when we live a fun life of joy and gratitude, rather than waiting until retirement to enjoy our days, we are rewarded with fulfilling and meaningful opportunities.

So.

How much time *do* you need to get started?

Honestly? Thirty minutes a day.

I promise.

Not that you'll make millions with "one simple trick!" or anything else you'd see in gross clickbait ads. (More on that, and why we feel slimy when it comes to marketing, in a couple chapters.) I'm just saying I really meant everything I said in the last chapter about simple actions compounding over time. A little bit goes a long way.

In fact, every single chapter has been part of a journey we've taken to get to this point:

- You've acknowledged entrepreneurship is for you (Chapter 1).
- You've faced a ton of fears (Chapter 2).
- You've agreed not to be a shitty boss for yourself (Chapter 3).
- And you've decided to take things one step at a time (Chapter 4).

So when you think about the life you want to build and what it would look like to work for your not-shitty boss, what do those steps look like *for you*? What kind of time do you actually have available, and what's the best way to use it?

I showed Amy how to dip her toes into a side hustle instead of that "go all in" BS. She worked through the course on her commute. And before long, her freelance writing had grown into a flourishing online business that took the place of her draining job and then some. She eventually was working only three to four hours a day and earning seven to eight thousand dollars a month. But most importantly, she got back thousands of hours with her son. She was able to create a day based on her priorities, no one else's. She is building her dream, no one else's. She's calling the shots.

Now, maybe you want to move at a quicker pace to get your business up and running. That's okay too, as long as you're not working unnecessary hours because you think that is what makes your work valuable. Or worse, because you're trying to live up to society's outdated standards.

There is not a set amount of time, energy, or resources that will guarantee success—mostly because the type of entrepreneurial success I encourage you to go for is completely dreamed up and defined by you. You get to choose what success looks like. You're calling the shots.

Instead of glorifying the hustle, focus on *your* goals, for just a little bit each day. Get to know your unique flavor of success. Start to imagine your ideal day. And slowly, steadily, you'll start raising the baselines needed to make that dream a reality.

Untangling Time, Money, and You

Have you ever done a "day in the life" thread on social media, or scrolled through someone else's? Like anything else on the internet, it's only a glimpse of reality, so you have to take it with a grain of salt. But scanning other people's days can be a fun way to start brainstorming what you want yours to look like. And they can be fun to post, too.

Not long ago, I posted an Instagram reel I called "a day in the life of a copywriter." It started with my seven-minute meditation first thing in the morning, then about fifteen minutes of reading. Then I made a cup of coffee and played with my dog before starting about two hours of work. Midday, I took a break to cook dinner ahead of time, then I worked another two hours and "clocked out" at three to go pole dance.

It was a pretty typical day in terms of my routine (and a seriously fucking awesome one, considering this is precisely how I designed it, and a testament to how far I've come). What's interesting to me is the responses I got.

Quite a few people were in disbelief. Some didn't think it was possible for them. And one person replied with a rant that culminated with how my day had been "too self-indulgent." He implied this was an impossible standard. He also couldn't see when any "real work" was happening (though I think he missed the four hours of work, since I didn't want to make anyone suffer watching me at my computer for that long—just like the unsexy training montages in movies). He dismissed my day as being unrealistic, then went about his life—probably without changing a thing.

A few years before, I might've been hurt by his message. After all, my fear of looking lazy (yep, self-indulgent) to my clients and students is what worked me into a panic attack in Bali. Now? I know his comment is a reflection of his own beliefs, and I love the life I designed way too much to let someone else's perception rattle me.

I've been in his shoes, too. Moments where I saw, I judged, and I walked off in a huff. But I've learned that these are the moments to get curious about. Because a strong reaction means something is rubbing up against your deeper beliefs.

It's an opportunity to examine and potentially question them. There's nothing wrong with deciding to keep your beliefs in the end, so you can't really lose anything by questioning.

And before I could really embrace my own ideal day, much less my own ideal business, I had a few key beliefs and expectations to work out.

You Decide How to Spend Your Time

On one hand, we're learning how to let go of old employee mindsets and replace them with the perspective of a business owner. On the other hand, being a business owner sounds like an all-consuming responsibility that few of us are ready for when we're just starting out.

Of all the people I've talked to about entrepreneurship over the years, women especially tend to see time as their biggest barrier. They have this belief that they can't be a good mom/daughter/sister/friend and a good entrepreneur—like it's obvious they have to neglect one in order to pay attention to the other. Moms especially hold on to this belief. Entrepreneurs miss out on their kids growing up, right?

They're workaholics.

They "do it all" in their business.

They always...

They never...

Listen, "they" will always exist. People who work sunup to sundown and have no life? That is one way of being an entrepreneur. But their work habits are more about them and their beliefs than the job—I know, because I've been in both spots. It's a choice.

For every person who never takes breaks, there's someone like Amy or me who learned how to scale back their hours (while driving up their income) in order to enjoy life more. And if your self-worth is tied to your productivity, this belief needs to be pushed back on first.

Isn't it wild how we can have the fear of turning into a workaholic sitting on one shoulder and the fear of not doing enough to be considered good or worthy on the other? And we're left stuck in the middle, frustrated. But here's the thing: the more you read stories like ours and get exposure to people living out the kind of entrepreneur life you want to have, the more you'll believe in your own possibilities. Without judgment.

In the meantime, it might still feel confusing, challenging, or impossible to spend another second on anything but survival. Realizing it's possible to be an entrepreneur without being a workaholic is one thing; doing something with that information is its own challenge.

In the last chapter, we started working on the mindsets that will help you start to separate time from money: microdecisions don't have to take up a lot of time in order to be effective. That's how learning new skills during commutes and making new choices at kitchen tables in rehab eventually got Amy and me out of our nine-to-fives—not jumping off a cliff and hoping we could build a solid business on the way down.

I want you to take those reassurances and start using them to dream.

In fact, make that your first goal—to spend thirty minutes a day working your way up to being able to set more goals. I'm serious: spend a half hour daydreaming about your perfect life *and count that as a business-building activity.* Not able to get there yet? Start with ten minutes, but make it consistent. Intentionally set aside time, and actually write your dreams down as they come. Not only will that small practice solidify your why and help you notice opportunities in alignment in your day-to-day life, but it will also give you a much stronger foundation to build from later on.

Once you have some ideals in mind, you'll be able to play with and explore the kind of life you want—the way you'll want to spend your time once you've got more of it—instead of trying to conform to what you think you're supposed to create.

Ultimately, we're trying to get your time back into your hands. Start by reclaiming ten minutes for yourself in the morning and see where that kind of agency and targeted personal growth takes you.

I know this practice is what has allowed me to work from home and set my schedule so I can spend as much time as possible with my family. Every day as a new mom is filled with gratitude for Past Sarah, who worked really hard to build a life where she could have meaningful work that paid the bills while spending serious quality time with my husband and son all day long. I get to see his contagious smiles every time he wakes up from a nap and hear his coos while I take a meeting or two. You can be a successful entrepreneur and because of that, make *more* time for your family or whatever else is important to you. It's totally, absolutely, 100 percent possible.

You Decide How to Earn Money

Is time really money? It *feels* true. Jobs pay you for your time worked—even salaried positions have an expectation of when you'll be available to them. If we're not spending time at work, we can't make money.

But entrepreneurship is not employment. Working more hours doesn't always earn you more money. And even when it does, getting paid hourly for your work keeps you stuck, attached to those hours in one way or another. No one can cover for you, you can't walk away, and except for raising rates, your earning potential is limited by the number of hours in a typical workday (plus whatever overtime you invariably have to work to make ends meet).

Time is our only truly finite resource, which does make it precious. Even when we think about compounding actions making our time "stretch" further with bigger impact, it's all metaphor. Time is limited, and if you build a business that's attached to the hours you can work, you'll have a much harder time finding the freedom we all craved when we started exploring this path in the first place.

The good news is, you have another, far more dynamic resource that can move you through time *much* more effectively than hourly pay: energy.

We've all experienced that feeling of flow, where it seems like you could go and go forever and don't notice time passing. You might even be exploring or building a business around whatever it is that made you feel that way. The kind of work that doesn't feel like work.

Then there are the times when you have to make one phone call to one draining person, and ten minutes later you're ready for a good nap and a solid cry.

See? Time is fixed, but energy is dynamic.

And when you find the kind of work that gives you energy instead of siphoning it away, you can't really charge by the hour anymore. I mean, you can, but there's no reason to.

Something that "feels like work" (read: hard and miserable) isn't worth any more than something that feels like a breeze. You don't win points for struggling. So learn skills that can make you more per project, while doing those projects in less time. Set your schedule around your energy flow and not just standard business hours.

Doing more energizing work gets you more and better results with less effort, so it'll feel like spending less time than the draining work, no matter how the literal hours pan out.

It's extremely difficult to manufacture more time to increase your earnings with hourly pay, but you can play with the dynamics of energy to maximize the use of your finite resources.

Untying your earning potential from time can look like learning a profitable skill, creating digital products, creating physical products, launching courses and educational material, and setting project rates instead of hourly. It looks like packages, promotions, and learning new skills.

It looks dynamic. It looks like whatever you want it to. A business like that has literally unlimited earning potential because there's no cap on what creative solutions you might think of.

I do want to be realistic here and say that there *are* periods of hustle as a business owner, and not all tasks are exciting and fun. There are moments of discomfort and times when you're stretching. There are unsexy training montages that no one wants to sit through. But those periods of hustle shouldn't last forever. They should be setting you up for greater freedom—more time, not less. I even have a little mantra I use during those periods of hustle. I remind myself I'm investing in future freedom by saying, "I'm building freedom. This season of hustle isn't forever." Because I'm not your "hustle forever" kinda gal, I need periods of rest, reflection, and refinement. And you get to call the shots, remember? If you're not that kind of person either, you don't have to stay stuck in the kind of energy you'll need to get you through growth phases and closer to the life you dream about.

When I first started working for myself, the concept of charging a project-based fee around what the value of my work was rather than the number of hours I put in was a total game changer—and quite frankly totally foreign to me. Even my last job, which was salary, demanded a certain number of hours for the pay they gave me. But copywriting is writing that gets people to take action, so it makes sense that you should be compensated for your skill—how many people you get to take action with your words—not the time it takes to write those words.

As I got better at what I did, I was compensated more, and my clients were also rewarded with better results. It's just like any craft, really. An expert carpenter is going to be paid for his ability to make gorgeous dovetail joints, and his client is going to be someone who appreciates that level of craftsmanship. As he grows in his skill set, his work won't be for everyone, and that's okay.

Eventually, when I decided to teach other people how to become copywriters, I created a digital product that could be sold over and over again, which further detached my earnings from the number of hours I spent working. Don't get it twisted—my program is anything but passive. It's gone on to take more and more of my time, and there have absolutely been periods of hustle where I've worked well over forty hours a week to get it off the ground or to make big changes. Most days, though, as a marketer and as a course creator, I've tried to only work from 10:00 a.m. to 3:00 p.m. And my income doesn't change either way, unless I want it to.

Just like you get to design the flow of your ideal day and the way you want to spend your time, you get to decide when you want to grow and when you want to enjoy what you've already accomplished.

No One Else Decides Your Worth

When we see someone making money as an entrepreneur, it's hard to know how much time they put in to get there, often because we haven't yet separated time from money. And when we do make that mindset shift, the next layer of work we uncover is usually about self-worth. Maybe *they* work less and make more, but could you?

(Hint: much of entrepreneurship is self-worth work, but the dudebros generally present such an inflated, egocentric version of self-worth that it can be a turnoff. It's okay. They're on their own journey.)

I can tell you all of this now, and I can remind you endlessly as a student, and I can get your attention as a friend, but you're *still* going to struggle through these phases of growth. You're going to get off track in a way that needs serious course correction. And sometimes you're going to make choices that look like they're off track but are exactly where you need to be. This is true for everyone. Because it's one thing to know something in your mind, and another to *know* it deep in your bones.

As soon as you start assigning dollar signs to your work, you'll be met with fear. Fear of how you'll be perceived, doubts around whether your work is truly worth that amount, imposter syndrome, and more. But if you get curious, you'll uncover those beliefs—some of which were ingrained in you as a child and aren't really yours—and you'll have the choice to shed them to grow.

I was raised to believe that extreme frugalness was a virtue, so I had a hard time spending money on tools, software, and hires that were necessary to take my work as an entrepreneur to the next step. I had the mindset that spending that money was taking money away from my bottom line, and I should be able to bootstrap everything myself. After all, that was the more noble route. In reality, those tools were business expenses that permitted me time to spend on the more complex and energizing parts of my business.

We all have different stories we tell ourselves. But the beautiful part about working through these beliefs through the personal development necessary to grow as an entrepreneur is that *this is the work*. It's work that will make your work-work *actually work*. And the rewards of this work are limitless. Personal growth makes your life more fulfilling, so it can't be put on the back burner. No more waiting to spend time on yourself until whatever is left over at the end of a grueling workday. You get to spend your prime energy on you. The first story you have to change is the one that makes you feel unworthy of that time.

The idea that time and money aren't the same has been cemented into meme status at this point. Artists often share something to the effect of "You're not paying for the thirty minutes I spent; you're paying for the ten years of learning and experience that went into it."

But that's the real kicker for most of us: not getting paid for our time means we're getting paid for *our experience and expertise*. For what we know and what we do. No wonder we feel like we have to run back to college or go after another certification. We've been conditioned to outsource our validation to perceived authority, and when we don't have the time or resources to access that validation, we second-guess ourselves. But here's the thing: even on the other side of that certificate, or even a PhD, many people still don't feel quite ready or qualified for whatever they've dreamed up next. Imposter syndrome still rages on.

If you've read other books like this one, you've probably heard the story about the man who felt so underqualified to be at a big event, which we all totally relate to...until we find out that the man is Neil Armstrong. Bad news for anyone waiting for imposter syndrome to go away once you're "qualified enough." Uncertainty in life is a constant. The antidote for uncertainty? Consistent actions that strengthen *self*-trust. Teach yourself to be your own authority.

Somehow, we've put so much value and worth into time worked and certifications earned that we've forgotten where the real value is found: in making a life we actually enjoy.

I met a woman in rehab—Josee—who was constantly being told to get a job in a gas station and just learn to be content with that. She didn't have a high school diploma, and given where we met, she had some stuff to work through, so people just wrote her off. The thing is, she was brilliant. I hired her to work with me on some writing early on. Before any of us knew it, her business had taken off.

There's no shame in working as a cashier, *if* that's what you want. But you should know that there are so many more options than what other people will say you're limited to. This is because experience and expertise aren't cultivated in the classroom, where we're used to finding our approval and qualifications. They're cultivated in the real world.

Plenty of people (most of whom aren't entrepreneurs themselves) are going to make comments and feed into societal messages about what qualifies someone to be an entrepreneur. In the early stages—and whenever you just don't feel like dealing with bullshit—avoid them. Sometimes it's even a good idea to not tell them what you're doing. It took me more than a year to tell my parents I wasn't planning on going to grad school but instead was pursuing freelance copywriting. I didn't know how to have that conversation with them while getting established was taking up so much of my energy. I couldn't chase my dreams *and* justify them to people.

Most of our loved ones, while really well intentioned, have no idea what they're talking about. The stronger your sense of self-trust gets, the clearer this will become. For now, if you're not sure what to make of someone's input, try asking yourself this first: "Has this person been where I'm trying to go?"

How close is their day-in-the-life to what you want yours to be?

If they're not all that similar, then their advice won't be all that helpful. Deciding who to listen to is part of the environment you'll create to set yourself up for long-term success.

A therapist shared with me a helpful image, one that she was using for sobriety but that also works well with a new business venture: "Think of your sobriety as a baby. You wouldn't take your baby to a bar, would you? You need to wait until your baby is more grown up before you bring them into the world."

Now, think of your business as a baby. If your business is still struggling to keep its head up and you're paying attention to it all hours of the day, it's reasonable to think that you'll need to protect that baby business from people in your life who are going to expect too much of your baby before it's strong enough. To give it space to grow and get stronger before stepping out into the world. Maybe they can support you and be part of your life in other ways, but they don't have to even know that you're starting a business. Not until you and your business are ready.

It takes a lot of work to gestate and birth an idea, and even when it's born, it's still so fragile and needy. Make no mistake. It's a privilege when someone shares their dreams with you. Even with the people I love most, I was apprehensive about letting them hold my son right after he was born. There was an overwhelming instinct to watch and make sure others were caring for my precious baby before I allowed myself to fully relax with them. It was the same with my business. I would put out feelers and make sure the people in my life could be a safe place before letting them in on what I was creating.

Protect your growing business from anything that isn't getting you closer to your ideal day and eventually your ideal life. It's just a baby idea for now—give it some time to learn how to walk around and feed itself before you start introducing it to the world.

And by world, I really mean your well-meaning but often unknowing friends and family members who are probably just going to reinforce the beliefs you're working so hard to undo.

Slow Is Fast

Whether you've got a weird relationship with time, with goals, or with your own self-worth, starting and running a business will *absolutely* bring it all to the surface. Trying to grow is going to highlight all of the mindsets that are keeping you from said growth. And those mindsets will run your day if you let them.

So how do you course correct when an old belief tries to keep you from getting to your destination? You have to name your destination, first of all. Otherwise, how can you really know what you're working on, how far you've come, or even which baselines to raise? Setting that "North Star" and "reconnecting with your why" can call you back in after you get caught up working more hours than you want to, taking clients you don't align with, or doing work you don't love.

But we've all heard that stuff before. What does it actually mean? Like everything else, we can start small. Just imagine your ideal day. A day in the life of *you*, but as a business owner. As an artist for hire. As an event planner. As a technology whiz. Whatever it may be. See the Instagram reel of Future You play out.

Now. Check in: Is the next part of your plan getting you closer to or further from that ideal? Or are you distracted by "shoulds" and making some misaligned choices as a result?

Time really is precious, so we're not going to take steps that make us miserable even if they look correct or productive to others.

We're all different people on different journeys, which takes us back to the beginning of this chapter: some entrepreneurs work nonstop and attract people who want to do the same. I don't resonate with that *at all*, and some people don't resonate with me. You may relate more to one or the other of us, but ultimately, you're going to find your own place on that spectrum.

Finding and owning your identity as a business owner is what matters, even if that requires trying on lots of different outfits until you find the perfect fit.

Dream until you can see your perfect day, then start to go after it, one step at a time.

Don't skip steps just to start making more money, and don't add steps just to look busy.

Let your business grow over time, at the pace that works to raise your baselines, not to slam yourself into burnout territory.

Watch for cues that something isn't taking you toward your ideal day. Course correct as soon as you notice the disconnect. *Say "no" often—and quickly.* Prioritize the clients and work that unlock flow, and release what drains you. Offload the draining work so that you're freed up to do more energizing work.

Make your own rules about how you work best.

The bigger your curiosity, the more likely you'll be to charge those ten-years-of-experience rates, deliver great work in less time, and start to live that life you dream about.

And if there's resistance to the idea of charging more in any way, the next two chapters are for you.

Let's do some "day in the life" dreaming right now. Take a moment to think about Future You. You're a thriving, successful entrepreneur who has crafted your business and life to be incredibly fulfilling. What does a typical day look like? Get specific and make sure to include how the elements that make up your day cause you to feel.

Here are some prompts to get you started:

What are your mornings like? How does this routine make you feel?

Write about your home, habits, and schedule. Do they make you feel empowered, peaceful, satisfied, etc.?

What kind of hobbies do you have? How does it make you feel to spend time doing something you enjoy?

What is work like? How do you feel in relation to the work that you do?

How else do you spend your time doing things that make you feel the most authentically you?

Now let's take a minute to reflect on the components of your ideal day. How many things did you list that weren't directly work-related? Maybe you wrote that you want to take time to exercise or cook nourishing food. Maybe you included having a morning coffee with a loved one or being able to pick your kids up from school. Go ahead and underline each one.

These non-work components in your ideal day that you just underlined are good indicators of what some of your core values are, things that are essential for you to feel fulfilled. Let's distill them down to a word or short phrase and create a list of these values. (Examples: quality time with family, daily exercise, time in nature, etc.)

Now go back to your "day in the life" and circle all the emotive words and phrases (especially the emotive words that describe how you want to feel about work), and write them in a list.

Let's pause and take in these two lists you just created. They're looking an awful lot like a North Star, wouldn't you say? On your wild journey of entrepreneurship, refer back to these lists often. Of course, we go through times of hustling hard and growth discomfort, but as long as you continue to align your life to your North Star, you can trust yourself to be moving in the direction of your biggest dreams.

I'm going to ask you to make one last list (for now). Write a list of ten things that would take you thirty minutes or less to accomplish that will take you one small step closer to having the life you described above. It can be as simple as watching a YouTube video or reading the next chapter in this book, or as big as buying a domain or having a conversation about your ideas with a supportive friend.

CHAPTER 6

YOUR RELATIONSHIP WITH MONEY

People who say money doesn't buy you happiness haven't given enough of it away.
—Joe Polish

Let's play a game.

It won't take long.

Get your notebook out and remember to take one step at a time—no cheating. Ready?

Write down how much money you want to make next year.

Don't think too much about it; just write down a number.

Got it?

Okay.

Now, I want you to double that number.

Really.

Pay close attention to all the thoughts you're having right now. Notice what comes up for you.

The good news is that, when you step into the world of entrepreneurship, your earning potential is placed squarely in your own hands—the sky's truly the limit.

The bad news is that, when you step into the world of entrepreneurship, your earning potential is placed *squarely in your own hands.*

What we believe about money influences everything. How we run our businesses, how we feel about ourselves as business owners, and how we interact with clients, customers, employees, contractors, and beyond.

For some, how they feel about money is a major limiting belief that stops them from even considering an entrepreneurial path—even when it would be the solution to all their problems and deliver on all their desires. But more on that later.

Right now, you need to know that what we believe about money directly relates to how much struggle or ease it brings to our day-to-day life. It changes the way we dream and how we go after that dream.

Unfortunately, our collective money mindsets suck.

If you're coming off of that exercise or even the last chapter feeling weird about imagining your perfect day, working fewer hours for more money, or charging literally anything for something you enjoy doing, you're not alone. So in this chapter, I want us to strip away all the stigma that feeds the fears, judgments, and worries that make money elusive. If we can do that, it'll be easier to see money for what it really is: simply a tool.

Seriously, we get so worked up about pieces of paper and coins that were only created so we didn't have to carry around spices and furs to trade. Money isn't inherently bad or good—the meaning we *give* to money is what creates its emotional context. And we're free to change that meaning whenever we want.

Money can be a very triggering topic for many of us. This chapter is a good space to practice getting curious if you get triggered.

Instead of immediately rejecting something because you start to experience big, scary emotions, try to figure out what those emotions are trying to tell you.

Challenge yourself to be open to reexamining your ideas around money.

At the end of the chapter, you have every right to wholeheartedly decide you'd like to keep your old beliefs around money.

What's most important is that you take the time to challenge yourself, because it's the best way to learn new things about your beliefs.

Don't Make It Weird

Money is like sex: an integral part of our lives that most of us were raised not to discuss. Both topics are taboo in many spaces. Fortunately, a shift to more open and honest conversations around money is on the horizon.

My parents' and grandparents' generations believed it was inappropriate (even rude) to talk about money, so I never knew how much the adults in my life earned. To ask them about their income felt equivalent to asking what their favorite sex position was. Yeah, I'm cringing too. You just didn't ask that kind of thing.

When I started paying attention to the ways people talk about money, I noticed how seriously weird we can be around things we're not comfortable with. I saw pretty well-off people pretend they weren't—often saying they couldn't afford things when they absolutely could or downplaying their purchases for no real reason.

And I caught myself doing the same thing.

After I started to earn good money, I made sure to point out when I found a great deal. I was constantly reassuring people I didn't spend money frivolously, and it was a *constant* source of anxiety.

Honestly, I wish you and I were actually having this conversation over dinner because that's exactly how I started to face my own issues with money. It came up the night Emily and I decided to go out for a "fancy" dinner, just because. Well, not *just* because. I was secretly celebrating my business crossing its first million in revenue, and I didn't even have the courage to tell my best friend.

We dressed up. We ordered lobster. And I was a mess.

Sitting there, I updated her about how well my business was doing—while covering my mouth and whispering. Why? Because someone might overhear, I guess? Because saying it too loud might jinx it? Because people might like me less if they knew I was successful?

Emily caught on to how uncomfortable I was, and she told me a story.

When she was little, her parents worked really hard to make ends meet. Both parents worked and her dad sometimes had to work two jobs to support the family of six. They lived in a little neighborhood on the bottom floor of a house that their grandparents owned, but to Emily, it felt like a castle. One day, her mom went out and got a huge box of Popsicles—Double Pops, to be exact. The brightly colored ones that had two popsicle sticks in them. And little Emily was sure they were rich.

Wanting to share her Popsicle wealth, she immediately gathered up all the neighborhood kids and made sure everyone had a Popsicle to enjoy. Within hours, she'd given them all away. It was a moment of pure abundance.

She vividly remembers the moment when her mom realized what had happened—Emily standing there with an empty box of Popsicles that she had just given away. She laughed while she told me how much trouble she'd gotten in, but Little Emily didn't get it—she was just excited to share with her friends. She couldn't interpret the defeat and frustration her mom had, so she thought she was angry at her. Little Emily interpreted that anger as *there's not enough* and *generosity equals hurting the people I love the most.*

In an instant, that moment of pure abundance was shifted into scarcity. A new belief was created, that there isn't enough to go around, and there's barely even enough for us. Once she had her own kids, Emily got it. Of *course* her mom had been upset. She'd splurged on something that could've been a treat for her kids for weeks, and it was all immediately gone. She understood that, after working so hard and wanting to bring home something special for her family, her mom was frustrated that her daughter had gone and given it all away.

And, Emily admitted, she could feel that Popsicle panic herself. When she took her kids back-to-school shopping and watched them throw their favorite little sweaters or pants in the cart, she would feel her anxiety rising. She knew her children didn't know how expensive everything they were throwing into the cart was. She even had feelings kick up that *she* would get in trouble for spending too much, just as she had gotten in trouble for the Popsicles.

She wasn't telling me the story to say she had it all figured out. Just that she understood why I'd whisper about my success. We live in a world dominated by a scarcity mindset. Where money seems limited and disempowering. Where money is vilified.

She added, "I've been thinking about how to get back to that place, honestly. How do we get back to that child-like abundance—so we can enjoy and share our 'Popsicle wealth' without panicking that it's all going to disappear?"

I immediately thought of my own childhood and my own story to share, though it felt kind of obnoxious compared to hers. (Then again, it originates in middle school, and who wasn't a little obnoxious in middle school?)

Basically, there was a trend in my school where all the girls were getting little starfish necklaces from Tiffany's. And I wanted one. I probably wanted to fit in more than I actually wanted the necklace, but it all felt the same to me. So I asked my dad for one. He told me that Tiffany's jewelry was not for children. That it was something I could buy for myself when I was a grown woman who had worked hard to earn it.

I actually appreciate the lesson today and totally get where he's coming from now, but at the time, I just really wanted to fit in like most kids do. My dad and I had a great relationship, though, so I remember thinking *that made sense* and pushing my desire for the necklace out of my mind. And just like little Emily, in that moment, a belief was created.

To paint a quick picture, my dad is a caring, generous, law-abiding citizen. As a teenager, I would often joke that he must have some undercover alias—maybe he was secretly a CIA agent or something. *Anything* to explain his highly virtuous ways. I found it impossible to believe that this man seemed to have no vices. My joke was that he snuck off to chain-smoke cigarettes. It stuck—every Christmas when we get together and my dad has to leave to run an errand, we mere mortals wink at each other and say things like "Sure, an 'errand.' Enjoy your cigs, dad." It's funny because it's so not who he is.

More seriously, my dad is a lovely, caring man, and so many of my beliefs around what it means to be good in this world came from observing him as a child.

I watched my dad as he wore pants until they were quite literally falling apart and drove his cars until the wheels seemed like they'd pop off and roll away. I vividly remember one of his cars was a Ford Explorer he purchased (I'm sure at a very good deal) from his brother. The driver's side door would fall off into your hand if you tried to open it, so he'd just climb through the passenger side.

Here's the thing though: he could have totally afforded another car. He made decent money, but he believed this was the *right* thing to do. Thriftiness and frugality had been instilled in him as a child, raised by parents who lived through the Depression. But as I observed this behavior, I turned it into a story about money itself: *Good people don't spend money on themselves, ever. Even when their car door is falling off.*

This behavior I had labeled as virtuous, paired with the story that you must work extremely hard to be deserving of nice things, created an impossible standard for me to strive for. No matter how hard I worked, I didn't think I deserved to have nice things. Even when I was purchasing a pair of much-needed jeans for myself (because the old ones had holes, just like my dad's), I'd get nauseous. Leaving them at the checkout and running out of the store.

Then there was this thought process: *Why would you spend $200 on something that you could find for $20?* Never mind the quality, durability, how it made me feel, or whether it aligned with my values *(hello, made in the USA)*. Frugality and scarcity trumped all.

When you judge something outright, it's impossible to have a healthy relationship with it. And the damage is often left unspoken...unless a friend catches you whispering behind a menu about the good things in your life.

Emily and I decided right then that we were going to face our weird relationships with money—her fears about scarcity and my beliefs about worthiness—and start building new beliefs. I'll tell you more about that later (spoiler: it includes getting matching Popsicle tattoos). But first, let's break down some of those beliefs together. Popsicle tattoos, optional.

Write a Letter to Money

Growing up, the adults in my life would rather tell little white lies than the actual truth because they thought keeping other people comfortable was the kind thing to do. But when we put on a show of frugality or stay modest about our earnings, we're not really making anyone feel better, and we're perpetuating a harmful collective belief. First, we're actually communicating (perhaps subconsciously) that we don't think the other person is capable of handling the truth. Then, we're agreeing with the unspoken judgment that having money is a bad thing, which reinforces the harmful narrative.

Good relationships are strengthened, not weakened, by honesty and trust.

So...are you ready to get honest? Try writing a letter to money as if it were a person.

Here's my old letter to money:

Dear Money,

Honestly, I'm so sick of thinking about you. I find you incredibly confusing, frustrating, and terrifying. I feel like you're always trying to fuck with me. Most days, I feel like I constantly have to check on you—to make sure there's enough of you. You're not reliable, and you can't be trusted. Sometimes we have fun, but I usually end up regretting those days. I am overwhelmed with guilt when I hang out with you. It's like you give me a hangover. Quite frankly, I'm sick of it. I don't want to have to worry about whether you'll be reliable. Ultimately, I'd like to not think of you much at all.

Sarah

This may seem silly at first, but it's a common exercise that is great for finding conflicting beliefs and often helps people identify how they really feel about something. We've kept those feelings quiet long enough—it's your turn. Write money a letter. Don't hold back.

Change Your Stories

Your brain comes up with judgments and self-limiting beliefs to protect you from harm. It's essentially made to be a fear-predictive machine in order to keep you alive. But because we live in a relatively safe world—at least compared to when our brains were forming—a lot of our fears are exaggerated or even imaginary.

This is usually where the fear of success shows up, which sounds totally strange at first. You want your business venture to work, right? Why would you be afraid of the thing you're working toward?

Then again, when you think about the way our culture relates to money, it makes perfect sense that we'd hold back at some point. There's a weird societal balance to strike between having enough and not having too much. If you step outside of those spaces, you're probably going to be judged, and to the part of our brains that exaggerates our fears, being judged can feel as serious as being exiled. Dangerous.

Getting a little more specific than "fear of success" usually hits closer to home, which is why writing a letter to money is a good way to spot your specific fears and beliefs, too. After you try that exercise, look at the words you used.

How many of these words made it into your letter?

Confusing	Guilt	Afraid	Manipulative
Frustrating	Mysterious	Powerless	Fun
Terrifying	Dependent	Abuse	Regret
Unreliable	Undeserving	Disappointing	Overwhelm
Not trustworthy	Evil	Exciting	Stressed
Greedy	Empowering	Confident	Calm

The way you talk about money gives you clues regarding the core beliefs you hold about it, and each of those beliefs affects the way you interact with it. Sometimes we're unaware of our money beliefs until we start paying attention to the things we say or the things we hear people in our lives say.

Just the other day, a friend was over and we were talking about charities and meaningful causes. He said, "Rich people don't donate hundreds of thousands of dollars to causes out of the kindness of their hearts. They only do it for tax purposes."

My ears perked up because, after years of working on my money mindset, I could immediately see how limiting this belief was. First of all, it is all-or-nothing thinking, which is so far from where the truth usually lies. Absolute statements are rarely true because we don't live in a black-and-white reality.

So, we know we're starting with a belief that isn't likely based in truth right out of the gate.

Second, this judgment is based on the "rich people are bad (or evil)" belief, which is pervasive in today's world. This belief keeps good people scared to earn good money, which not only keeps them poor but is so incredibly harmful to the collective.

Think about the kindest person you know—wouldn't you prefer they have substantial wealth? Because you know they'd do good things with it, right?

This is where many people's fear of success originates. If you're concerned about being a good person in this world and you believe having money makes it impossible to be a good person, then you'll stay small to fit the cultural definition of *good*. Meaning we're collectively perpetuating the very problem we have with wealth distribution in the world.

Third, this mindset takes those who are wealthy *and* doing good in the world and pushes them underground. That leaves us with far fewer examples of wealthy people doing good things with money, which reinforces the original belief *and* keeps people hiding their kindness in the shadows. We even have a shaming tool called "virtue signaling" that we can weaponize against them if we'd like. We've created a powerful belief loop that keeps good people small and afraid of success, and quite frankly, it's hurting all of us.

Reallocating wealth to good people is one of my primary drivers and why I am so freaking passionate about showing how attainable entrepreneurship is.

If I were in charge of allocating wealth, I'd much prefer a mother who's sitting at her kitchen table agonizing over choosing the right supplier based on how they treat their employees to some twenty-something dropshipping bro sitting on top of a Lambo. Those guys are literally taking advantage of the fact that we believe money = evil. We're harming ourselves with our money beliefs without even realizing it. (I'm using caricatures intentionally here. Obviously, there's more variety in this world, but you get the point.)

See if any of these beliefs about money resonate with you, either for yourself or what you've heard from people in your life:

Rich people are greedy.

Rich people are bad.

I can't make money and be a good parent.

I can't have a lot of money and be a good person.

My relationship with my family/friends will change if I earn good money.

People will think I'm a sellout if I'm wealthy.

If I'm successful, I'll make people insecure.

Usually, but not always, our core beliefs can be traced all the way back to childhood, which can be a tricky conversation to have. I can't even guess what your life was like as a kid, and I have no idea how comfortable you are talking about those years now.

You may have had parents who sat you down and talked with you about money. Maybe you had an allowance or job(s) at an early age. Or you may not have been educated about money at all.

Some of us love talking about and unpacking our younger years. Some of us avoid even thinking about it. The one thing we all have in common is that we're not kids anymore, and it's time to decide which of our parents' beliefs we want to hang on to and which beliefs we need to release because they are no longer ours.

Speaking for myself—but I think you can relate—it's okay to think critically about the impact our parents had on us and still know they meant well. We're all just doing our best, but limiting money mindsets run deep and are reinforced by the culture at large.

When I first examined my core beliefs around money, I realized I judged wealthy people. Hard. I thought if you were rich, you were probably greedy or self-centered, especially if you did anything that demonstrated your wealth.

Only extreme frugality could be virtuous.

Now, you already know where that belief came from. And since I do too, I found a way to tackle those broken beliefs in a playful way. When recurring, protective feelings show up, I like to name them something silly that detaches them from the belief I'm trying to change. So, when I really need to combat the feeling that spending money is irresponsible, I'll call it *Dad*: "It's okay, Dad. I am actually happy with these jeans." It's a quick reminder that not every belief came from me or is one I want to keep. And because I love my dad, I have a better sense of compassionate curiosity about that belief instead of getting caught up in self-judgment. Perhaps most importantly, it makes me laugh and brings levity to the whole scenario. And couldn't we all use a little laugh?

Self-criticism makes us critical of others, and vice versa. And those beliefs can show up in the weirdest ways, seemingly unrelated to the original event. Case in point: a person in my life was an antique dealer, and I judged her and her clients *so* deeply. Without realizing what was happening or why, I would actually find myself disgusted with how they were spending their money. How could anyone spend thousands of dollars on a chair when there's more important work to be done in this world?!

Somehow, I wasn't seeing my own contradictory beliefs. It touched on my Tiffany's necklace belief that these choices were frivolous and irresponsible, but I also believe those pieces are works of art and that art is important.

When we're unwinding core beliefs, we have to look at both sides of the coin. If I'm judging people for making their lives beautiful, I'm probably judging myself in the same way. And I'm only limiting myself because of it.

Just in case you're not feeling ready to tackle self-judgment: remember that judgment keeps us from having healthy relationships *with everyone*.

Let's make that a little more concrete: if I'm judging people for dropshipping crap on Amazon and moving to Bali, I'm limiting myself in some way too.

Yes, I've judged the shit out of bropreneurs in this book—mostly because they are an easy caricature to represent a collection of ideas and behaviors. There are extractive people using the Amazon machine just to benefit themselves, without concern for the consequences of their actions.

But there are also people with incredible stories about feeding their families, getting out of debt, and growing beyond belief—thanks to dropshipping. And when people solve their initial financial stresses, they are free to think bigger. Because they are no longer surviving, they're thriving…and you know I'm a fan of that!

If I were sitting with someone over dinner, listening to their personal stories about finding some freedom through Amazon, I'd be thrilled. Who am I to say they did it "wrong"?

One person's investment in a business path they find accessible or in things they find beautiful doesn't have to make sense to me. I don't get to sign off on every person's use of money. And since we're looking at both sides of that coin, that means no one else gets to sign off on my use of money either. I don't have to be understood in order to appreciate myself and the beauty, love, and freedom I bring to the world.

Let's stop gatekeeping our own success, shall we?

Name New Beliefs

Today, one clear reminder that I've made a shift in my money mindset is that I buy quite a bit of handmade jewelry and art. I get to support artists I love while enjoying beauty without beating myself up for it. I appreciate craftsmanship and adore creativity. Enjoying their works of art is a privilege I don't take for granted.

You'll find your own clues that you're healing, but let's get a jump start on it right now. Go through each line of your letter to money and look for the negative words that clue you in to old beliefs you'd like to heal. Make a list, and then write down positive alternatives. Google searching "antonyms to [your words]" can be helpful. Here are some to get you started:

Unreliable - Abundant	Stressful - Comforting	Disappointing - Joyful	Guilt - Dignity
Manipulative - Clarity	Abuse - Healing	Afraid - Curious	Confusing - Simplicity
Regret - Confident	Overwhelming - Inspiring	Powerless - Empowering	Dependent - Independent
Awkward - Confident	Undeserving - Worthy	Stressed - Calm	Greedy - Generous

Now, try turning some of those words into new beliefs. Here are a few examples:

I am worthy of making more money.

Money comes more easily to me when I'm relaxed about it.

I know money is an infinite resource.

I can make good money and still be honorable.

Money is abundant and I am open-minded about new ways to bring it into my life.

I make money by working smarter, not harder.

Shift Your Energy

Money is just part of the energy we exchange with each other, but most of our parents viewed (or still view) money as a direct connection to force instead of flow. They taught us to believe the harder you worked, the more money you earned.

This certainly applies to some extent, but lots of us are making money according to the value of our creations or skill sets which doesn't necessarily depend on the amount of time we spend each time we sit down to work.

There's a modern parable that goes something like this... A factory comes to a grinding halt because a piece of machinery suddenly stops working. The business is losing a million dollars a day due to this unforeseen issue. They call a mechanic who specializes in this machine to come fix it. He walks up to the equipment and pushes a red button, which restarts the machine, and it's business as usual. He hands the business owner a bill for ten thousand dollars. "Ten thousand dollars!" the business owner complains. "You just pushed a button!" Calmly, the mechanic explains that the owner isn't paying for the time it took to complete the task but the knowledge and expertise needed to know exactly what to do as efficiently and effectively as possible. The price is backed by the six years of education and fifteen years of experience necessary to know to push that red button. Without the mechanic's knowledge and experience, this business would go on to lose millions of dollars each day. So, was this action worth ten thousand dollars? Absolutely.

This mindset shift changed my life. Why? Because it shows why we should price our work based on value whenever possible. Which makes our earning potential exponential.

When you put energy out into the world—whether it's time, talent, skills, or efforts—that energy can return to you as money. And this energetic exchange isn't always linear. In fact, in the world of entrepreneurship, it's usually not. When you untie your earning potential from your time, the whole world opens up to you.

You don't have to earn millions of dollars a year to make money a positive experience. That might not be your desire (and remember, you get to decide what you want and go after it). It's definitely not what I wanted when I started this healing process. But if you want to make more money at all, you have to stop hating it. Resenting money is a surefire way to make your life as a business owner (or, you know, as a human) infinitely more difficult.

Let's take a step back and look at a few examples of the energy we can give money:

How would it feel to make an extra $300 by helping a friend's new business get off the ground and running?

How would it feel to make $500 by selling a beautiful piece of art you've poured your heart and soul into to someone who adores and appreciates it?

Both of those situations would feel great, wouldn't they?

Here are a few more examples of the energy we can give money:

How would it feel to make an extra $300 by lying to someone about the details of something you're selling them on Craigslist?

How would it feel to make an extra $500 by covering up significant damage to the car you're selling to some unsuspecting stranger?

Feels gross, right?

It's easy to see the energy shift in each of these situations. Even though we think of "making money" as good or gross in different circumstances, it's not the money that's the problem. If some money feels good and some feels gross, it might help to remember that money itself is neutral. It's the energy behind the exchange that we actually notice.

Money gives you options. It gives you power. It gives you flexibility and control over your life.

Money is what we make of it.

Money only has the meaning we assign to it.

Money amplifies what's already there. Good or bad.

You might see rich people doing bad things, but thinking money is evil doesn't affect those people. It only hurts your relationship with money and impacts the likelihood of more of it coming into your life. Jeff Bezos doesn't give a shit about what you think about him. But thinking all wealthy people are bad keeps good people poor and more money in his hands.

I want more money in the hands of good people.

In fact, I'm willing to bet that the world would be a better place if *you* had more money.

I was working with a mentee once, and she had a gorgeous list of things she wanted to do in this lifetime. A recreation center for underprivileged kids was one that really stood out to me. She had such a vivid vision for how this would look, and yet she had such a strong belief that having money was bad. This belief was so strong that she didn't allow herself to save any because that meant she had more than enough. But as soon as I painted a picture of how her virtuous dreams required the very thing she resented, she quickly saw how her money belief was at odds with the good she wanted to do in this world. And the mission became undoing this belief so she could be the change she wanted to see.

Like kid-Emily's impulse to give away all of her Popsicles, I bet you're constantly thinking about what's good for other people—even if you're also feeling mom-Emily's anxiety about where the money will come from. Being worried about taking too much or having too little are most likely rooted in your concern for other people, and that's exactly why you're the kind of person we need to get "rich."

And by the way (*checks notes*), women in general tend to donate more than men.

It's not just donations that count, either. Making your business work for you allows you to send more of that good energy out into the world in all kinds of ways. Here's a small example. Thursday is my favorite day of the week because that's the day my housekeeper comes. She's an absolute delight and does a damn good job. As we became more financially secure, we decided to pay her more. Just because we could, and because we wanted her to know how much we valued her. She had also been telling us she wanted to take classes in the evenings, so we were excited to give her that gift.

The energy I bring to my work can be exchanged for enough money so that I have more to exchange for her energy—and her energy creates so much joy in our household that I'm happy to exchange more than most for it.

Another time, a friend went through a nasty divorce and wasn't able to afford her kids' school during the expensive proceedings. We were able to jump in and pay for their school so their life would be less impacted by everything that was going on. So they could still see their teachers and their friends.

Being able to show up and support people in my life is one of my big WHYs in entrepreneurship. And I have to add that I definitely got this core value from my parents, who are always supporting people in their lives profoundly, both emotionally and financially.

Just a few years ago, I would have been so worried to share stories like these for fear of being shamed for virtue signaling. But I've seen behind the curtain. It feels great to be able to pay the people in your life more. To support your friends and family in times of need. The rich people who *don't* do that—the Scrooges of the world—are operating from a scarcity mindset. They see money as a finite resource that they have to hold on to. While many of the wealthy who live in abundance probably fly under the radar because, well, you know…

Scarcity is a hard mindset to let go of. In Emily's Popsicle story, her mom wasn't wrong for being upset when they disappeared in an afternoon. Technically, the Popsicles were a finite resource, and it was hard to see where more would come from. Emily's complete childlike sense of abundance kept her from feeling any of that fear. Both Emily and her mom were driven by love for others, but an abundance mindset allowed Emily to lean into that love without any reservations. Because she wasn't worried about how the Popsicles got there or whether they'd ever come back, she could chase her impulse to share.

The powerful side of doing personal mindset work around money is that you start to see it come into your life more easily. Abundance *becomes* real.

Know Your Worth

Over and over again, I've seen the way core beliefs can either hold people back or skyrocket their business and life. I've seen mindset shifts become the key to business growth. I've seen the way someone elevating their self-worth results in higher income. And I know we're getting a little spiritual here, but I am half hippie, half scientist. I would be holding back some of the most important discoveries I've had on my quest for a more fulfilling life if I didn't touch on the energetics of money. (Plus, we're not hiding behind taboo anymore—this is my personal truth, and I'm not going to keep it from you.)

Getting really clear about the stories you have around money is essential to making changes in your life, pursuing a life of entrepreneurship, and freeing yourself from the limitations of old mindsets and ways of working.

This is an ongoing process, not a one-and-done exercise. Once you start asking questions and inviting more self-awareness into your life, you'll start to pick up on more fears and limiting beliefs that need to be unpacked. I'm *still* uncovering self-limiting beliefs around money. The work of personal growth never really stops; it just evolves.

The night Emily and I talked about our weird issues with money, we both realized we weren't alone. We also realized we weren't stuck in those mindsets.

I didn't have to whisper about my business—it was doing exactly what I worked so hard for it to do.

I didn't have to buy cheap Amazon shirts just to save money—having fewer items from local creatives was more in line with my values, even if the price tag was higher.

That night, Emily and I made plans for a "weekend of abundance."

We went on our version of a shopping spree. We got our matching Popsicle tattoos. We held hands and breathed through the anxiety in checkout lines. We reminded each other that we weren't being financially irresponsible. We made each other take the tags off of what we bought right away so we couldn't return anything in a panic when the buyer's remorse set in. It was pretty hilarious.

And a week or so after Emily got back home, I got a package in the mail.

It was a Tiffany's starfish necklace. I promptly burst into tears, surprised at how emotional it made me.

The thing is, I wasn't ever ashamed about how well my business was doing. I was ashamed of myself for enjoying and being proud of it—all of it. The success, the lobster dinner, and the starfish necklace from Tiffany's were all in the same category, and I didn't think I deserved any of it.

This is such a common core belief that I want you to work on it first and foremost (and forever!). *You deserve an abundant life. Period.*

My husband, Ben, laughed at me recently when he overheard me begging a woman on my team to let me pay her more. She started out because she saw a need and wanted to meet it. When we saw how much she was helping the people in our community, I reached out and brought her on officially, and she's been part of the team ever since.

We were on the phone that day because she was weeks away from having a baby and had no plan to take time off after the birth. She was still undercharging and had completely maxed out both the rate she could charge and the time and energy she had to bring on any other clients. Her work was high value and people were lining up to work with her, but she didn't have the capacity to grow with the systems, pricing, and mindset she had in place. When the baby came, she was going to be completely stuck without any way to take a break.

I told her she could tell me to back off if I was overstepping, and then I asked her about her client load—who she was working for regularly, how much energy they took up, and what she was making with them. It didn't take long to see that she had shifted out of just editing (fixing written content) and into coaching (helping the writers improve). Helping people get better is worth way more than simply fixing typos. She was essentially offering coaching and not charging for it.

We also saw that at least one of her clients was more draining than the others. When it came to that work, she was miserable. That work took longer and felt more frustrating than anything else she was doing. It was energetically draining. I suggested she drop that client and let me pay her the amount that she'd been getting from them as a retainer. That way her income would be covered after the baby came, and we could give her a more enjoyable workload at the same time. I saw her value—and I saw a younger version of myself as well. She reminded me of myself seven or eight years earlier. The version of me that was scared to raise my rates, scared to overvalue my work, and getting caught up in imposter syndrome even though the demand for my work was at an all-time high.

Take a step back and examine your business. Run the numbers, look at the costs (even when the cost is emotional, like a draining client), and decide what makes the most sense in terms of fulfillment and profit. It can be *so* hard to take those steps for yourself. Especially if you don't know you can make choices simply because it feels better. Like firing a difficult client. That one change can free up a tremendous amount of energy.

She didn't see herself as a coach just yet; she saw herself as an editor, confined to standard editing rates, and the flat rate I was suggesting as a "raise" took her outside of market rates for per-word editing. She couldn't wrap her head around charging that much.

I wanted to pay her what her work was worth.

But she had to believe her work was worth more.

I knew she had the ability to change people's lives while still enjoying her own. I wanted her to realize that potential right then, while she still had a baby to enjoy, not years down the road.

It took over an hour for us to shift from problem-solving around maternity leave to begging her to let me pay her more, to her finally seeing in herself at least part of what I saw. Every time we talked about Write Your Way to Freedom or Let's Build Your Online Business, she had big-picture ideas and so much excitement around the business. She was constantly providing value and contributing to my business in seriously valuable ways—and if she didn't have to spend all of her energy grinding out literally pennies at a time, how much more value could she create?

To be fair, I am still uncomfortable telling you this story, even though being able to pay people well is one of the reasons I wanted to make more. Self-deprecation, not celebration, is my comfort zone. But I want you to see what it actually looks like for me to have a human-centered eight-figure business. It looks like creating opportunities and helping others grow through what I've been through. It looks like encouraging people on your team to grow. It looks like parental leave and conversations about self-worth. And sometimes it looks like encouraging them to venture out on their own, even when it's not the best thing for me or my business.

I don't want you to be afraid of raises or even six-, seven-, or eight-figure success for yourself, because having a good relationship with money is having a good relationship with your life. If you're expending all of your energy killing yourself on work that barely gets you by, to the point that you have no way to take time off with your new baby, something is off.

I wanted her role on my team to grow; I knew that having more time and energy freed up would allow her to show up more fully for our community. As a person who loves seeing people grow into their power as entrepreneurs, I knew that the only thing stopping her was mindset.

The amount of times I've heard people say they're "finally charging what they're worth" is both encouraging and frustrating. Yes, I want you to charge more. Yes, I want you to see you're worthy of it. But really, your worth as a person stretches way beyond money, period. *You* are invaluable, no matter how much energy you have available to exchange. You are charging what your **work** is worth.

Separate who you are from what you do.

See yourself more clearly. Know your inherent worth. Then you can see the work more clearly, start to charge appropriately, and welcome the abundance when it starts to flow in.

Before we move on to marketing, take another moment to journal about money. Your answers can include lessons you learned through things people have said or done to you (direct) or observations that you've made (indirect).

What are a few direct and indirect things you learned about money from your dad (or caregiver or role model)?

What are a few direct and indirect things you learned about money from your mom?

Were any of these things you learned about money contradictory?

What do the people in your day-to-day life say about money?

What emotions would you experience if someone asked you how much you earn?

What emotions do you most often associate with money?

What are some of the words you associate with money?

Did your parents or role models teach you about money more directly or indirectly? Maybe you picked up on the stress and anxiety of never having enough, and so you worry about money even when there *is* enough.

Did you learn that there isn't enough money to go around?

Did the people you interact with most often judge wealthy people? Would it be scary to earn more if you knew the people you love most think rich people are bad?

What was your earliest experience with money?

How did you observe people dealing with money?

How did you have to earn money?

Did you get paid for babysitting or mowing the lawn?

Did you volunteer your time consensually, or was it demanded of you?

What did it look like if you wanted to purchase something out of the ordinary?

Were you encouraged to get your first job?

What were your motivations for earning your first paycheck?

Now take a moment to think about your core values.

What are the most important things to you in this world?

Spending time with your family?

Being able to travel often?

Creating art that you love?

Would money help you achieve any of the dreams you just mentioned more easily?

What would your life look like if you could see past your limiting beliefs?

How would you feel? What would you do or stop doing? What would be different?

Last, let's take a quick moment to translate your own goals, availability, and values into some early goals for money.

Ready? Here's how it goes:

- How much would you need to make in order to live in alignment with the values you just named and the dreams you've been identifying throughout this book?

Maybe you want to travel the world. Maybe you want to replace your income and work from home. Maybe you want to replace your partner's income. Maybe you want to pay for a kid's extracurricular activity.

Whatever it is, get it into number form: how much does that version of you need to make in a month?

- Now, break that number down.

Let's assume you're going to work five days a week—roughly twenty working days in a month—unless part of your dream is to work less.

A common number I hear at this step is $200-$300 a day, but yours may be more or less.

- Last, connect that number to the industry you're in or thinking about building a business in.

Think about what you'd need to do in your business to hit that daily number. If you make gorgeous, handmade ceramic mugs, how many mugs would you need to sell? If you write blog posts, how many would that need to be? If you're a virtual assistant, how many clients do you need to have?

You may want to do some industry research at this step, because your first idea of what your service or product is worth may be lower than reality—it usually is.

More often than not, people are surprised to discover that it's much easier to create a sustainable income with their passion than they realized.

To check your math, start calculating the time it would take you to serve those clients or make that product. A gorgeous, handmade, hand-painted mug doesn't need to be and shouldn't be priced as cheaply as possible. They are art and take actual blood, sweat, and tears to produce, so be sure to account for that.

The most important thing here is you've got some real targets to work with. All too often we have ideas around starting a side hustle or a business, and we don't sit down to crunch the numbers and figure out exactly what it's going to take to untie our time from money.

When you break it down into daily and monthly goals, you give yourself a goal that also leaves room for flexibility.

You might have some days you earn more or less, and it won't happen overnight, but as long as you're taking baby steps in generally the right direction, you're getting closer and closer every day.

I want to share one last story with you about one of my students—Cassidy. Let me set the scene for you. In September of 2019, she came to my first in-person event. She had just had her highest-income month to date: $4,607.50. Cassidy was as a new business owner, and she had already doubled what she was earning in her nine-to-five. So, she had already doubled her income by choosing entrepreneurship. Which she found exciting but also really scary and intimidating.

I walked her and the other attendees through the exercise at the beginning of this chapter. I asked her to write down how much she wanted to earn next year. Her hand was literally shaking as she wrote down $100,000. It felt impossible; it felt so big. Then I asked her to double it. So, she had to write down $200,000. She told me her brain was like, "No, no, no, no, no, there is no possible way I could ever make that much money!" That exercise showed her all of her limiting beliefs around what's possible.

Three years later, at another event, I reminded her of this exercise, which led to a really funny realization. In her memory, she thought that I had asked her to 5x her income! I reminded her that I had only asked her to double it, which made us both laugh. That number felt so big to her at that point in her entrepreneurial journey that she was sure I had her multiply it by five.

And you want to know what the best part about this story is? She is well on her way to actually earning that much money. To be earning $200,000 a year, you need to be earning about $16,600 a month. And she has had multiple $20,000 months. So now that goal, which only three years ago felt outrageous, is well within her reach. And that is the power of pushing back on your limiting beliefs.

It's like the story about Roger Bannister, who was the first person to break the four-minute mile. Everyone said it was impossible to run a mile in under four minutes before he did it. But then when he broke it, he shattered limiting beliefs for so many. In fact, a mere forty-six days later the record was broken again. And since then, over a thousand people have run a sub four-minute mile.

This is how powerful our beliefs are and why this work is so freaking important. So please don't skip it. Dig into it and know that the discomfort is so, so worth it.

CHAPTER 7

FIND HEALING THROUGH MARKETING

Time to face the music.

To acknowledge the elephant in the room.

To swallow the frog.

Insert more "do the hard thing" idioms here.

It's time to talk about marketing.

Ads, especially in the US, are literally everywhere we look. You can't even put gas in your car without a commercial blaring at you from the pump. (Side note: did you know that's not normal in other parts of the world? We're so used to the marketing onslaught that it's like ringing in our ears: annoying, we wish it would go away, but for the most part, we just live with it. What can you do?)

The more ads there are, the more big-time marketers have to compete to get above the noise, which makes more ads—and some of those ads are getting increasingly invasive, misleading, and *weird*.

But nobody (that I work with) wants to play that game. The annoying and weird ads stand out because they are, well…

annoying and weird. Marketing that's in alignment with its target audience feels right and therefore doesn't feel like most people's definition of marketing. Really amazing marketing goes unnoticed.

I tell it like this: if you found the cure for cancer, you'd still have to market it.

And if you don't market it, or you market it poorly, even the best, most effective, most needed medicines (which are *products* too, by the way) will be rejected by entire groups of people. Even people who desperately need them.

Similarly, as an entrepreneur, if you don't have clients or customers, it may not be because you don't have an amazing product or service. You may not have customers because you aren't effectively marketing or you're not marketing at all.

I can't tell you the number of times I've come across creatives, changemakers, and business owners who aren't marketing the amazing things they're doing simply because they don't want to morph into the sleazy used-car-salesman caricature. But I can assure you, that worry is precisely what's going to prevent that from happening to you.

Remember, you're here because there's something calling you to be your own boss. This is all about getting your mind right to be a business owner and to be a better boss to yourself.

And you can't have a successful business without good marketing.

I know it's not a favorite subject for many, and honestly, ten years ago, if you had told Past Sarah she'd have a career in marketing, she would have scoffed at what seemed like an impossibility. Marketing was cringey. Marketing was salesy. Marketing was dishonest. These are just a few of the stories I had about marketing swirling around in my brain.

In my quest to find meaningful, location-independent work, I came across copywriting. Actually, I started in technical writing because that felt more palpable to my self-righteous beliefs at the time. But I was quickly bored out of my mind. With a serious dose of skepticism, I started reluctantly looking into copywriting.

What I quickly realized was that we are surrounded by copy. Copy makes up most of the words we come across on a daily basis (outside of the books that we read). And I quickly realized that *excellent* copy actually went unnoticed. I'll take that one step further: excellent copy and great marketing are genuinely enjoyable when they're meant for you. But because "delightful marketing" didn't fit my limited idea of what marketing is, I didn't categorize it as marketing at all. Falling into the confirmation-bias trap, I rejected anything that didn't fit my story.

As my eyes began to open, I came to see marketing as powerful, necessary, and wonderful when done well.

Now, I love to teach people how marketing is a superpower we can use for good.

It's been a long road, folks.

If you want to be your own boss, the marketing conversation is one we have to have. How you approach this one aspect will make or break your business growth. Even if you aren't thinking about growth yet—well, you're here, aren't you? Growing your business starts with boring montages and unsexy microsteps, remember? You're growing *right now* just by reading this book.

We're not going to focus too much on the actual steps of your marketing plan in this chapter (mostly because the details will change a month after this is published anyway). Instead we're going to focus on growth, and how all of this work you're doing to invest in yourself is going to make your business stronger and more resilient. Just like you.

Because, as I see it, if you think marketing is gross, it's just as limiting as thinking money is evil. And these beliefs are dangerous because they keep good people from doing incredible things in this world.

I hope we can all agree: we need good people—just like you—empowered to have a bigger impact.

Now that we have my chapterly call to take over the world out of the way...

(Good) Marketing Doesn't Feel like Marketing

Before we go any further, let's define what I mean by marketing. I simply mean an intentional and consistent promotion of your services or products. Bonus points if there's a good strategy in place. However, what that strategy looks like will differ depending on where your audience is hanging out online and what your personal preferences are.

My beliefs on marketing differ from most because I don't think you should do anything you absolutely hate. And there are a lot of "shoulds" out there that lead people to mistakenly believe things like *You must post on social media three times a day to be successful.* I promise, I'd never make you do something you hate, because I won't do something I hate. Plus, we're here to create a life that we love, remember?

BUT.

First, we have to make sure we don't have outdated or misinformed self-limiting beliefs creating friction.

Genuine alignment is not the same as forcing your life to align with old beliefs.

Maybe you're holding back because you think marketing's gross. I definitely did.

Maybe you're dealing with another layer of core beliefs—just when you thought you were ready to make money without feeling greedy, now you have to ask people to *pay you money*? Uh…

Our work in the last chapter was to start identifying those limiting beliefs, and that work won't ever really stop. Each level of growth reveals another layer of healing. Our work in this chapter will be to start healing those limiting beliefs—specifically, through your relationship with marketing.

Just like money, we can point to both good and bad examples of marketing. We can avoid the kinds that feel terrible and go after what feels aligned with our values and goals.

But avoiding marketing altogether "because it's gross" is never going to be the answer.

When I say we're going to heal our relationship with marketing, I don't mean we're going to get okay with being obnoxious advertising machines. You don't have to have a loud, cheesy commercial at the gas station, you don't have to litter your web presence with pop-up ads and clickbait, and you definitely don't have to become social media famous (unless you want to).

To get a better idea of what I mean by good marketing, I want you to think about a product or service that changed your life. One that you didn't find through word of mouth. (Although, that's technically marketing too. *Great* marketing, actually.)

How did you find that thing? How did it find *you*?

Was it an ad you scrolled by?

A blog post you found on Google or on social media?

A post from someone you were following? A post from someone you weren't following?

It probably wasn't a commercial, pop-up, or billboard.

It might take a second to remember because when good marketing is done well, it doesn't feel like an ad or an interruption. It feels authentic and genuine. It feels like finding something that's meant for you. It feels like connection. It feels *good*.

Like the time the Instagram algorithm sent you the exact pregnancy pillow you needed when you were in your third trimester and couldn't get comfortable at night.

Or the workout program you signed up for because a friend shared a post by their trainer who got you following them.

The conditioned belief that marketing is gross (and that anything that isn't gross can't be marketing) becomes a filter on the world, so that only the annoying interactions stand out. But you know you can dig around on Instagram for the thing you need, knowing that the algorithm will bring you all kinds of ads for it—basically doing your shopping for you. Creepy? Totally. Convenient? Also, yes.

You think of marketing the thousand times a day you're clicking a tiny X or driving by a billboard or switching off of a commercial—not the time you hopped on a call with someone and they pitched you their program and you bought it, and it changed your life.

Your vibe attracts your tribe as they say, and the Write Your Way to Freedom and Let's Build Your Online Business communities are perfect examples of this idea played out through marketing. I call this world-building marketing. It's marketing that brings people together around a common idea, belief, or goal. It's powerful, and it feels good.

World-Building Marketing Creates Loyal Customers

I often say that good marketing is playing the long game, but it really isn't a game—it's a commitment to building a business that has genuine impact and that cares about people, the planet, and profit. Anyone can create communities, missions, and even whole worlds with marketing. Make no mistake, when people convince others to join an important cause, they are using effective marketing. When people use meaningful, thoughtful marketing, the natural byproduct is loyal customers.

It's estimated that companies lose $136.8 billion per year due to avoidable customer churn, meaning businesses generally aren't taking good care of their people. This is especially unfortunate since acquiring a new customer is five times more expensive than selling to an existing customer.

In fact, the success rate of selling your product or service to someone is (on average):

- 60–70 percent to an existing customer
- 5–20 percent to a new customer

Meaning we should be taking better care of our people.

Additionally, loyal customers are (on average):

- 5x more likely to repurchase
- 4x more likely to forgive
- 4x more likely to refer
- 7x more likely to try a new offering

Good marketing connects, delivers, and keeps people coming back for more.

(Good) Marketing Feels like Connection

I would have never made it in the *Madmen* days.

Gone are the days when the customer is always right or the old-school transactional view of work keeps entrepreneurs promoting and selling nonstop in order to keep people coming in the "door." That dynamic is exhausting for the consumer *and* the marketer.

People care more about who they buy from today than ever before, and the internet allows us to know those companies and brands more intimately. This is a good thing. Especially for you, the growing entrepreneur. It's exactly why I've come to love marketing so much.

Because people expect, respond to, and thrive on connection, you get to use marketing to build authentic, lasting connections with the people you want to work with.

Marketing just gets the word out about what you do. "What you do" is the way you make a living, can elevate your life, and can start to give back in meaningful ways. And when you get to bring real people into that very real experience, the whole process of growth through marketing can feel aligned with your larger values and goals.

You can choose who you want to call in. You can lead with value. You can cultivate connection around the thing you do. These are the factors that create loyal customers, help you outlast the competition, and even create new friendships along the way.

Feel-good marketing is world-building. You're showing your audience the world you're dreaming of and inviting them to stick around for a while.

My students consistently tell me how they felt like the ad that brought them to my programs was speaking directly to them. They often share with me how grateful they are that they stumbled across that ad—sometimes at 3:00 a.m. after a night of tossing and turning, worrying about life.

Then they asked me what my strategy was for writing it.

The truth is I just wrote it as if I was talking to Past Sarah, the version who was desperate to escape her nine-to-five. And when I wrote an ad to the version of me who was searching for solutions, I connected with thousands of people who felt the same way.

Infused into all of the marketing for my business are my ideas around living a life with more freedom, with family and friends at the center. We are always talking about writing for brands that bring us meaning, so work feels less like work and more in alignment with our passions.

I could have just built a course, sold it, and allowed people to figure it out on their own. But I've seen the power in people connecting over a shared mission, facilitated through products and services. We've built a community centered around these values. The result is when we get together in real life each year at our annual event, everyone feels like old friends. Like we've known each other for years.

Inside of this world I've built (using ads, don't forget), we are connected through shared ideas, beliefs, and emotions. Our group has a distinct feeling, uses a distinct language, and has a distinct tone. We are a tribe that inspires each other, lifts each other up on rough days, and helps each other out when we're stuck. The empowerment we create together, inside of that space, stretches far beyond anything I could have offered in a commoditized product.

Now, you might be thinking it's easier to create world-building marketing around my program because it's a group of people on a similar journey, but I've also built online worlds for my clients around their supplements, their products, and their philosophies. One community was for people starting and enjoying the keto diet. Another was for people who loved nerding out about the gut microbiome. And one was for people who were interested in mindset work and personal development.

Consumers are demanding world-building, connection-centric marketing from businesses and brands at this point—I know I am. Sleazy marketing techniques don't work as well (not that we want them to). Generalized marketing might work for huge brands like Coke or Nike to try to capture anyone and everyone, more or less shoving the product or service down our throats, but for most of us? Mass marketing and poor marketing can create resentment—either for the bad-fit customers who are unhappy with the product or the uncomfortable experience with the brand. It's like starting a relationship off on the wrong foot.

Plus, businesses that only focus on bringing in new paying customers lose over time: it's *far* more expensive to find new customers than to convert people who are already familiar with you.

Good marketing is more like matchmaking: trying to pair a specific product or service with a specific person who could use it. When you find that person and communicate to them what you offer and how it will make their life better, it doesn't feel like marketing for either of you. It just feels like a good match.

Marketing can and should be human-centric. When you focus on people over profit, the money ultimately comes. And if you let it, the process can be life-giving and even healing.

You Set Your Own Strategy

Marketing is a whole industry in itself, with countless tools and techniques and all kinds of competing schools of thought about what works and what doesn't. So if you're feeling like you have to do it all right away (or ever), remember *there are marketers who market marketing*. Don't buy everything they sell you—not every rule, strategy, or tool will be a good fit for everyone.

Case in point: I think branding is overemphasized, in general.

Yes, it helps to have a professional website, and a professional website needs to have some sort of aesthetic. But the great thing about branding is that high-end aesthetics are minimalistic. You don't need a lot of complicated features *at all*, much less in the beginning. Initially, your business is your deliverable; everything else can come after you've established yourself a bit and can afford bells and whistles.

For the first three years, my logo was a Canva-made icon of a feather quill. Not some amazing looking feather, either—it definitely looked like '90s clip art. And I did just fine. I focused on the program and the transformation above all else, which is really what matters first and foremost.

The same principle goes for naming your business or setting up "an identity." Don't waste time trying to be cute or clever, and don't waste money trying to be perfectly polished. Name your business based on what it is (*Your Name + Service* or *Product*) and call it a day. Move on to serving your people. You can always circle back and change it.

That's my approach, anyway. It might be a controversial one, but it's worked so far. Not only for me but for my students. It's all too easy to get hung up on planning a logo and printing out business cards, but I remind them time and time again that those things are not what make you an entrepreneur. In fact, they're a distraction. Fancy procrastination, as I like to call it. Most branding can wait.

The bigger point here is that you can start from wherever you are, with whatever you have available to you. And usually, you have one of two things available to spend when you're starting out: time or money. Some things take more time but less money, and some cost more but don't have to take up as much time.

Time-Spenders: Social Media and SEO Content

Time is always precious—but in the beginning, it can sometimes be easier to find than money. It's important to consider balancing not only what's financially expensive but also what's time expensive. Here's what "time expensive" might look like:

Posting on Instagram every day to increase your reach.

Creating helpful YouTube videos.

Writing long-form Search Engine Optimized (SEO) content for your website (basically how Google finds you).

Each of these are powerful, relatively cheap things to DIY, but they cost a lot of time.

Even if you have time available to "spend," you may have other reasons for shying away from this kind of content creation.

I'll be honest, being visible online hit a huge, deep-seated fear in me that I was coming off as an attention-seeker.

As a writer, I managed to avoid being in the spotlight altogether. I was writing for other people, and I found those people with a website and cold emails. That was enough to build an annual income that hovered around $300K—no social media *or* paid ads required. When I chose to step into marketing for my course, I had to get uncomfortable. I've never wanted to be "online famous," or even well known. I only started creating content for my own business because I wanted to help more people.

At first, the only way I could get myself to show up was on live Q&A sessions for my students—something that felt undeniably helpful to people. Eventually, I felt barely comfortable enough to start creating YouTube videos answering the most common questions people asked me. *Barely*. Again, the thing that got me out of my shell was the feedback I continued receiving that what I was creating actually created results for other people.

Say what you will about external validation; without some positive feedback from my audience, I would have never kept going.

But then, my tolerance for visibility grew so much faster than I expected it to.

I'm still not Insta-famous or anything, and I don't plan to be. But the thought of going viral doesn't give me hives anymore, even though I still don't like watching my own videos. Sharing my knowledge and expertise online is actually fun and exciting now. (Well, most of the time.) The initial anxiety that I used to feel is gone, and I am amazed at how quickly that change happened.

This process taught me two really important things.

First, that confidence comes from taking action. It was the process of showing up every day that grew my confidence. If I waited around until I *felt* confident, I never would have started in the first place.

Second, that you do not need to do *everything* to be successful. Initially, I tried all the channels: Reels, YouTube videos, blogs, everything. I thought I had to do it all. I signed up for so many free webinars on social media growth that I had to abandon the junk email account I used for them. I finally realized the most important thing is to pick one you can do *consistently* and somewhat enjoy, then double down on it. Take it from me: you will make yourself crazy trying to do it all.

Now, I don't say any of this to say you have to "just start" and maybe one day you'll get comfortable. I want you to know that I gave myself permission to grow through the discomfort at my own pace, and I'm giving you that permission too.

You can have a successful online presence without ever showing your face (remember Emily's slime venture, from Bet Your Bottom Dollar?). You can post content but refuse to watch it (I've still never watched one of my YouTube videos). You can pick and choose what kinds of content you post.

And if you get full-body cringes like I did just thinking about marketing your business, take some time to figure out what beliefs you're bumping up against, and grow your business in another way while you're working on growing yourself.

Money-Spenders: Paid Ads and Influencer Marketing

If you have money to set aside for advertising, you don't have to spend the time (or emotional energy) on content creation. Paid ads let you promote your product or service without bombarding friends and family or spending time on a blog strategy.

This is the route I chose to introduce more people to Write Your Way to Freedom and Let's Build Your Online Business. I chose paid ads because I wanted to continue to hide behind my computer as much as possible. So I saved money for my first launch, wrote a few ads, and built a funnel. Now, this little ol' sentence actually packs in a lot of work. It took a few months to learn all the tech, plus a few months of getting it all up and running. So it's by no means the easy way out or completely time-free, but it did allow me to grow more quickly and with greater certainty.

I spent $2,000 on ads with my first launch and earned $4,579. And I quickly realized another benefit of paid ads: once you nail down the process, you can predict, "If I put X number of dollars into ads, I'll see an X return on that investment." I *loved* this predictability. And, as you already know, I also loved that it didn't require me posting on social media every day.

Another growing form of paid marketing that takes the spotlight off you, isn't time-consuming, but costs money, is influencer marketing. I'm sure you've noticed the people you follow on social media promoting products or services they love—that's all it is. I don't have much experience with this form of marketing, but I know people have had incredible success through connecting with influencers to promote their products for them. It's yet another option in the sea of opportunity.

Real quick, I want to touch on spending money to make money. Because a lot of people initially have resistance to spending money on their business, even when it's on something that will result in a greater impact. This is an example of an employee mindset holding back a business owner.

I once was helping a friend with her website for her business and recommended she pay for a template and some professional photography. She was totally open to the idea but casually mentioned the reason she hadn't done it before was because she "didn't like spending money to make money." This statement caught me so off guard. Because in my mind, spending money to make money is one of the easiest and most reliable ways to earn money. It's quite literally what marketing is.

Let's go back to the example I gave of my first launch. For every dollar I spent, I essentially got two back. Now, if someone were to tell you that they could double every dollar you have, what would you do with all your dollars? You'd say, "Take all my money!" It's a no-brainer. This is the power of a return on investment in marketing.

But I get it. The "I don't like spending money to make money" mindset is a deeply ingrained belief that comes with being an employee. When you view your money as your income, and it's tied to the number of hours you spend working, plus you think in terms of saving rather than investing, every dollar is precious. If someone has been earning $15, $20, or $35 an hour, it makes sense to think like this. The problem is it doesn't take into account the cost of your (even more precious) time. Any investment you can make to save yourself time and grow your business is the better move. And this doesn't mean you have to be infinitely growth-minded in a Wall Street sense—just quite literally start working smarter, not harder, until you find the right balance of time and money for you.

As an entrepreneur, you have to—*absolutely have to*—start thinking like a business owner. So ask yourself: what tools and resources will give you your precious time back so you can reallocate it to your zone of genius? Because even if you go the more time-consuming route for your marketing (hey, that might be part of your zone of genius!), there are still going to be elements of your business that would benefit from becoming a business expense.

Use Marketing to Heal Yourself

You might have noticed, but I'm a big believer in outreach. Because the simplest way to reach people is to *reach people*. I know a lot of people like to glorify the idea of attracting people with their marketing, but quite frankly the fastest way is to reach out. To ask or to share what you're doing starts making waves in the universe. It communicates, "I'm ready," without just waiting around for it.

I'm going to sound biased here, but copywriting and marketing are skills worth learning, no matter what approach you expect to take. Long before I taught it, *learning* marketing appealed to me because of how it connects people. Understanding what makes copy good is essential for all business owners. And it's not hard to learn *or* do, especially when you're generating your own copy for your own business.

Once you have the basics of marketing down, growing your business through marketing gets a heck of a lot easier. In fact, it's why so many of my students eventually go on to take everything they learned and start another business venture: a charter sailing company; autism programs; home goods; pregnancy and postpartum programs; home improvement businesses; nonprofits. Because they were able to venture deeper into entrepreneurship, they understood what it took to launch and run a successful business—any business—through marketing. Because knowing how to sell your product or service is essential to *any* business's success. Because copywriting is more than just writing; it's understanding how marketing strategy fits together and how to implement it well.

Once you know how it all works, for example, growing an email list and sending a few emails can cost next to no money and have a profound impact on your business's growth. And because you're trying to make a match with someone who needs what you have to offer, you can have a lot of fun scouting for details that will help you make a great connection.

Whenever I sit down to write to Past Sarah, it's like I'm calling back to myself ten years ago:

Sarah…this is Future You talking to you; here's what I want you to know…

Especially early on, this was a powerful healing exercise. I started with a pain point I felt when I was struggling the most, and I wrote about what I know would have helped me out of it. And then I wrote about another pain point. And another.

One by one, I wrote my way through things that I once thought I'd never make it out of. And I offered a way out. I offered hope. I offered things that actually helped me grow and heal.

The amazing part of this approach is that the people who tell me my ads spoke to them don't look just like me. "Past Sarahs" have been in their fifties and wanting to finally take time to write after spending a lifetime following someone else's path. They've been sons who wanted to take care of their mothers. They've been single moms and bachelors. But they know the pain I'm talking about, and they want that hope too.

And if anyone reads what I've written and doesn't feel like it "spoke directly to them"? That's okay with me. I'm not looking for those people. In fact, good copy *should* repel the people it's not meant for. I want to find all of the Past Sarahs out there who are days away from hitting rock bottom and help them find a better path.

When you write from that angle, it taps into such a deeply human impulse—to help someone who's struggling in a familiar way—and everything else becomes less important by default. Perfectionism, the fear of rejection, worrying about what to say...

Here's what's crazy about it all, too: I genuinely care about every person I reach out to, and I want the best for them. I bet you do, too. So when we spend all day sending that message out to *our past selves*, we're healing little parts of ourselves over and over again.

And before you think that only works for teachers and coaches and actual healers, go reread Emily's slime story in Bet Your Bottom Dollar. It doesn't take a serious product to enable serious healing.

Remember: Marketing Isn't Personal (Even When It Is)

Even after hearing me talk about all of the ways they can build their marketing strategy around what feels good for them, aligns with their values, and helps someone with a thing they've overcome, students still tell me, "I don't want to sell myself."

I'm sorry, what?

Where does that come from?

Better question: what does it *mean*?

It sounds so grim, like we're selling our souls or something. You just need clients and customers, you don't need to sell your kidney on the black market.

Listen: I know marketing feels like putting yourself "out there," but *you're* not what's for sale. No matter how genuine and personal your marketing is, there's a difference between your value and worth *as a person* and the value and worth of *what you're creating* for people. And until you can separate what you do from who you are, marketing will always feel overwhelming. An unsubscribe on your newsletter will feel like personal rejection. Views and comments will feel like personal scrutiny.

I'm not saying marketing is or should be easy. I'm just saying the stakes aren't as high as we make them out to be.

We're going for personalized connections with people—not merging your personal value with what you do. That's the kind of people-pleasing mindset that had me working a million hours in my early days. And the thing is? Overidentifying with your work and productivity actually makes you more *dis*connected from your clients. It doesn't serve anyone.

I've seen a few variations of the way "nobody cares" can be taken as sad and nihilistic, or it can be taken as "nobody cares, *whee!*" As in, nobody is really paying attention, so there's no reason to take it too seriously.

By the way, just because I advocate for marketing as an important skill to learn, that doesn't mean I think you need to learn it to be successful or that your copy needs to be perfect. Or that anything has to be perfect.

It's so easy to obsess over getting something exactly right. But if you look around, you'll notice plenty of people who have spelling errors, weird logos, and basic websites. And a lot of them are crushing it.

At this point, I consider my typos to be a form of rebellion against perfectionism. People love to call me out on them, but it just reminds me how far I've come—and how those mistakes haven't ever held my business back.

Plus, every angry or snarky comment about a typo gives that ad more engagement and makes it perform better. So, thank you, grammar snobs.

The thing is, those "gotcha!" comments and DMs aren't personal either (though sometimes they can be worded like they are). When someone takes time out of their day to criticize someone else for a minor mistake, it says more about who *they* are than the person they're criticizing. What a waste of their precious time. Successful people are not calling people out about their grammar in comments on social media. They ain't got time for that.

We've spent a lot of time talking about how you're building your business for your dreams on your terms in your way. But when it comes to marketing, this part of your business is not about you at all. It's about offering people something that they might need. And not everyone you reach actually needs what you're offering. Maybe they just don't need it *right now*. It isn't personal.

Your cold email isn't going to ruin your recipient's day. No one is going to stew over how *not-exactly-perfect* your product was for them. People aren't clicking the X on your ad and making up stories about how much they hate you. And someone who is a perfect fit for your service isn't going to walk away *because you have a typo in your email.*

You can't lose the right person over that stuff. And, if you're working on that abundance mindset, you know you can't ever run out of the right people. Just keep experimenting. Keep learning. Keep growing and healing. Keep playing!

None of this is as big or scary as we make it out to be. Not any of it—the marketing, the business building, the taking a chance on yourself.

Stepping out on your own means you call the shots. You decide what a win looks like and how you want to get there. You decide whether you're slowly easing into the deep end or diving in, sink or swim. You decide how and when and where you want to be seen or heard.

And all of *that* boils down to one thing: you're the only thing in your way.

I'm not saying this to mindset gaslight you—this is more an invitation to start taking steps forward, no matter how small. No one else gets to tell you you're ready or not ready.

I do want to give you a heads-up that you never really "arrive." Each time you unlock a new level—most clients ever, highest income yet, biggest day of sales, craziest quarter, new product—you get to tackle self-limiting beliefs all over again. Feelings of perfectionism and imposter syndrome and fears of success and vulnerability will come back in new, sometimes surprising, ways.

Every new level of personal growth you reach gives you access to new potential business growth. And the doors that open from *that* success usually trigger new layers of personal growth, which gives you access to more success, and... It's a spiral that can hold you back all over again or can launch you to levels you haven't even imagined yet.

So if you felt like you were making headway with the money chapter, but some of those same feelings are popping back up at the mere mention of marketing—congrats for making it to the end of the chapter. And hang in there because this work doesn't stop. But the growth that comes from it can be oh-so rewarding.

We're stretching into new spaces as a rule, not an exception.

Think about a real-life person who has loved what you have to offer, who you've helped, or who you've impacted in some way.

Usually, when people tell me these stories, they get a little emotional. It's easier to see how important your work is through someone else's eyes. Telling me about someone else's experience breaks down that resistance we all feel around "selling ourselves" and reminds you why you're offering that product or service in the first place.

So take a minute to write about or just sit with the idea of that person while we work through the following questions because reaching them is the important thing, not whatever idea you have of marketing that you're learning to reframe.

You might also use that story to create some new affirmations:

I am more than my work; I am inherently valuable.

What I have to offer matters.

(Add yours.)

Now, imagine telling that person you're never going to provide that product or service again.

What would they say to you?

How would they try to convince you to keep going?

Write those things down and put them in a place where they are visible while you're working on marketing tasks.

That person, as well as Past You, is who you're writing to. That's who you're buying ads for. That's who will see your name come up over and over again until they click *and they'll be so grateful that they did.* Whenever you're feeling weird about being visible or feeling scared about all of the "what ifs" that might happen, look at that list and remember two things:

- There are other Past Yous who still want or need what you have to offer.
- Future You can take care of any "what if" that might happen.

Everything else to do with marketing is just the practice of putting yourself in front of the right people over and over again, and it'll feel a little bit better every time you do.

CHAPTER 8

MAKE YOUR LIFE HAPPEN

While I'm not trying to be a "manifesting babe" any more than I want to be a bropreneur, the truth is, I want you to see what you can create once you've shifted your mindset toward growth, abundance, and all of that incredible dreaming we've been doing.

When you intentionally keep what you want top of mind, you start to notice things in your life that will help you get there. This is because your brain is a powerful pattern recognition machine, noticing similarities and reoccurrences everywhere. When you intentionally keep what you want top of mind, you engage a part of your brain called the reticular activating system (RAS).

This special bundle of nerves at the base of the brainstem is responsible for our wake/sleep cycles, fight-or flight responses, and most relevantly filtering the subconscious from the conscious mind.

In other words, the RAS works hard to highlight important information, and *we get to tell it what's important.*

Yes, it's part manifesting. But it's also really well-documented.And it really does look like magic.

I'm convinced this is how I met my amazing husband, Ben. He cringes a bit when I say that—like I created him or something. But all it really means is that when I started looking for him—really intentionally defining what kind of person I was looking for—I finally found him. I wrote out a very specific list of qualities and traits, all the way down to how he'd be more active than me, with dark features, and how he'd be intimidatingly brilliant and profoundly kind. Because all of this was top of mind, when I found him, I thought, "There you are, Peter." Though he didn't get the Hook reference, so we had to sort that out.

It's also how I found our home in LA.

When people find out I moved from the mountains of North Carolina to Los Angeles, they generally want to know the story. They're so dramatically different that there's got to be something interesting that happened behind the scenes, right?

Not really. I just needed to be around the kind of ambitious energy that LA is full of.

Small towns in NC are a "bring your own job" kind of place for most people—where you're not likely to find a lot of opportunity, but if you have the right pieces in place, you can create a lot of quiet stability. The lifestyle is much simpler there. You can work as a bartender and make enough to go mountain biking every weekend, and for a while, I loved living that life.

It's rich in nature and community (exactly what I needed to recover, yeah?), and I always imagined I'd be drawn back to it again after I'm done with my business-building ventures.

But in between? I needed the energy of a big city and a big change.

So I made it happen.

Then I met Ben—and *then* we found our house. One that made even skeptical Ben ask if manifesting was real.

The first time we found the listing, everything about it was perfect...*except* that its Zillow post was two years old, and it was not on the market. After months of joking to everyone who would listen about how we were going to one day buy "the Spanish house" (named for its terra-cotta roof shingles), Ben sent me a new listing to consider. It had so many features of the Spanish house that we loved, except it was all white-washed and modernized.

I almost didn't realize it was THE house until I saw its distinct gate. Turns out, some guy in tech had bought it *as a gift for his girlfriend*, whitewashed it, and then they broke up. We were the first people to see it and made an offer immediately. This became our home for the next three years. The way it came into our life was so serendipitous that even skeptical Ben asked, "Is this what manifesting is?"

I'm not saying these things appeared simply because I wanted them. Instead, I've learned that when I put very intentional ideas out into the universe, work toward them, and stay open to how and when they'll appear, strange and wonderful things happen.

Our beliefs have a profound impact on our reality.

That's what I mean when I talk about making your life happen. Putting something top of mind so that your brain starts looking for it. Then you start making connections and noticing opportunities so quickly that the thing you're looking for seems to just appear. Right out of thin air.

This is the difference between manifesting and wishing, and I don't want anyone to get caught up in the kind of "manifesting" that keeps you feeling stuck where you are while dreaming so far out into the future that it feels unattainable.

So instead, I prefer to think of it in the way that I opened this chapter: making the next part of life happen. Or, *the framework for getting shit done.*

Put it out into the universe, start to take action, course correct along the way, and watch what kind of life you can create.

How Minutes Move Mountains

I get weekly emails from people saying that the mindset work is the most powerful thing I've taught them. Some of my favorite stories include a wife who finally grew her confidence and danced with her husband in public for the first time in over a decade. Or the mom who implemented her practice with her teenage daughter who was battling cancer, then saw her shift into a happier, calmer energy almost overnight. And the guy who shared with me that he was finally able to build a business because the shame of having moved in with his parents temporarily was no longer crippling him.

That's why I had to write a mindset book. Because the details of building a business are going to change, and when you're feeling confident, inspired, and hopeful, you'll be able to navigate those changes with confidence. But without this foundation? All that's really left of entrepreneurship is the hustle.

So what have we learned so far?

In **Chapter 1**, we talked a lot about possibility, but I also asked you to start looking at why you want to build a business and what might be holding you back. Now that we've spent some more time together, go back over your answers (or answer them now, if you skipped it—I see you). What has changed? Where do you see yourself going now? Do the obstacles feel as big as they did in the beginning? Do they feel bigger because you're dreaming bigger?

In **Chapter 2**, we started to think about goals—not what you think you have to do, but what you actually want and need to do. Take a look at those goals again. Dig deep, past what sounds virtuous to say, to get to the core of who *you* are and what matters to you.

What haven't you permitted yourself to name out loud?

Now, what if you started your day with those goals? Write down your value-aligned objectives for the day. The week. The future.

Get specific enough to connect each goal to how it will feel. The brain creates memories based on emotion, which is why smaller traumatic experiences are so sticky and formative—because your subconscious never forgets. (It's also why serious, big-T Trauma can sometimes be forgotten, even though it's just as formative. Your brain wants to protect you from them.) So if your goals aren't yours or they're disconnected from any kind of emotional payoff, they'll probably fade away.

Name them in a way that makes you feel excited for your future or proud of yourself for living out your values. Instead of "I'm earning $8,000 a month," try "I'm proud that I've built a business that earns me $8,000 a month. I'm able to put aside money for savings, and this makes me feel financially secure."

In **Chapter 3**, I gave you some affirmations you can use to grow beyond the boxes you might feel stuck in. You built your own at the end because sometimes affirmations that someone else writes can feel a little off or like they aren't real. If you haven't done that yet, go back and write a few that come from you, your values, and your goals.

Sometimes affirmations can feel unbelievable precisely because they are touching on your biggest fears. If you're having a hard time connecting to your goals and affirmations because the fear is loud, try to just rephrase the fear: *I am stretching into new, unfamiliar, uncomfortable territory, and that's why I'm outgrowing my shitty job.*

Another powerful way to grow into your dreams is with gratitude. If that feels cliché, remember Andrew Huberman? Check out his podcast, *Huberman Lab*—in particular, an episode called "The Science of Gratitude & How to Build a Gratitude Practice." About twenty minutes in, he calls out everyone who's rolling their eyes. He knows we're out there thinking it's fluff, but the science behind gratitude is strong. He calls it "the biggest hack you can use to improve your life," and says that one too many of us skip it because it feels too easy and a bit woo-woo.

In **Chapter 4**, we demonstrated how small daily actions compound into profound growth. So try journaling through these steps every day for a month, just to see how you feel at the end of it. Adjust as needed after the month is up—but don't lose the momentum you've created.

Keep up the habit of making room for yourself every morning, just like we talked about in **Chapter 5.** If you're writing down your own goals and affirmations every day, you're tapping into what you really want and keeping your brain on that path.

Other things you can commit a little bit of time to and still catch a big payoff include working out, reading, friendship, and hobbies. We think these kinds of things have to take an hour or more, so we put them off "until we have time." But the truth is we always have a free ten minutes here or there—we just don't set intentions around how we'll use those minutes because we don't see the small steps as significant enough.

Don't forget that cutting things *out*—stopping whatever doesn't serve your goals—and saying "no" is just as important as saying "yes."

Name something that's essential to you and figure out the smallest increment of time you can devote to it, then set aside that amount of time every day. On your calendar. Make it happen because every minute you spend investing in yourself is worth it.

And *you* are worth every minute you spend investing in yourself.

We worked through a lot of money blocks in **Chapter 6** so that you could embrace how much your work is worth, but I can't tell you enough that *you are inherently invaluable.*

If you don't have an affirmation to latch on to yet, there it is. There's so much power in communicating worthiness and belief in yourself, even if it's just a glimmer of belief that you don't feel yet.

Chapter 7 asked you to start thinking about taking your business to the world, but don't miss the part where you don't have to feel ready yet. You can market to the parts of yourself that are still healing. As you start creating the life that you've been dreaming of, you can also create the world that your audience is only just starting to imagine.

When you make life happen for yourself as an entrepreneur, you make life so much better for everyone else too. You build entire worlds.

There's so much to work through in every chapter of this book, but you can recap it all with a simple morning routine. You don't have to start your day at 4:00 a.m. or go to the gym at the crack of dawn or anything else like that. Build the day you want to have, but make sure it includes these steps:

- Write down your gratitudes, and really feel the energy behind them.
- Write or rewrite your value-aligned goals (with emotional language, in present tense) for the day, the near future, and the far future.
- Write a few affirmations that directly counterbalance any fears, negative self-talk, relationship issues with money, and procrastination.

This can all seem so simple that it's easy to skip. Just like movie montages, these actions will barely make the final cut, but this is where you become the champion you were always meant to be.

A Whole Life to Build

As you start to experiment with ways to make your dream life happen, don't forget that your literal environment—who and what you're surrounded by and how you interact with it—is just as important as your work successes (or more). Hobbies, friends, and real-life interactions are all part of that environment.

As an entrepreneur, your whole world can wind up in a computer before you know it. But the number one indicator of human health is strong human bonds. This shows up really clearly in "blue zones" (the areas all over the world where people live to be 100 or older).

Lots of studies have been done on these areas, trying to figure out the commonalities that change life expectancy so much. And the clearest answer is human connection. Strong relationships are far better for your health than anything else you can do.

The kicker: you *deserve* to build that whole, long, happy life.

In the darkest season of my life, my therapist told me he wasn't surprised I was depressed: "You're living completely out of alignment with your core beliefs. No wonder you're miserable." He helped me look around at the path I was on and acknowledge how many of my day-to-day choices were in total opposition to the life I actually wanted. Then he helped me start making different choices. To this day, he's one of the most important people in my story.

For the longest time, I didn't think I deserved anything at all.

I bet you've created a lot for other people, in your previous jobs or in your family. Women especially tend to take care of everyone else first, then give themselves what's left. To the point where it's easy to forget you even have needs, or that something like free time for your hobbies can be a need. Even when you finally break away to take some time for yourself, feelings of guilt creep in.

There's a famous study about rats and addiction, where only the rats in boring cages used the morphine available to them. Rats with exciting spaces didn't feel drawn to it at all.

Hobbies aren't a luxury. They literally give you life.

And no, whatever you're building can't replace the things that give you life. That's not something you'll hear in the entrepreneur space very often—bropreneurs especially like to talk about the job *becoming the hobby*. They're weirdly proud of it, just like they are about being the lone wolf. I love my career, and in a lot of ways it lights me up like a hobby would. But it's not my only thing.

I've been obsessed with mountain biking, pole dancing, sailing, farming, microbiology, epigenetics, sexuality, and entrepreneurship. How's that for a mixed bag of interests? People often ask how I have so many hobbies, which is always a surprising question for me. My answer? Just...try things. Push yourself outside of your comfort zone, often. The longer you isolate, the harder it is to build experiences and relationships into your life. So get out there and get messy. And if you need to, call yourself out for being awkward as you try. Everything is easier when you don't take yourself so seriously. Have a good laugh along the way.

Put it out there into the universe that you want to make friends, find a hobby, or do something silly. Start actively looking for opportunities to do those things, and then when they show up out of thin air, try them!

We are multipassionate, multifaceted creatures. Embrace how dynamic you are. See your messiness as the gift that it is. Stretch, a little more each day, toward becoming your fullest self with your absolute best life.

You are allowed to have fun.

You are allowed to hate it and change your mind.

You are allowed to cultivate different aspects of yourself.

You are allowed to completely change directions.

You're never too old.

And it's never too late.

Where else can you permit yourself to be fully YOU and fully enjoy your life?

Write yours here:

I'm allowed to...

I'm allowed to...

I'm allowed to...

I'm allowed to...

I'm allowed to...

Now write down a few hobbies that you want to try—it's okay if this is the first time you're actually admitting some of them! Think small (like making homemade sushi or hiking with your kids), and think big (like learning martial arts or how to play an instrument). Write them here:

Which one is lighting you up the most? Circle it! What is one small thing that you can do today to begin making room for implementing it in your life? After all, showing up and not giving up so that you can have these moments of living your best life is what makes it all worth it.

CHAPTER 9

WHAT COMES NEXT?

Most of what I do these days is teach and mentor new entrepreneurs through my online programs and in-person events. And about 60 percent of my teaching time is spent on mindset work because that's what actually holds people back most of the time. One of the reasons I wanted to write this book is because I related to so few people who teach the skills of entrepreneurship in today's world. I've spent the last decade sifting through advice and pulling the gold nuggets that resonate out of the heaps of broesque advice that doesn't.

But the other 40 percent is still important—the skills, the action, and the movement that comes with just doing the damn thing. It's reminding myself and others that, "Yeah, taking the entrepreneurial path can be hard," but it's the right kind of hard. It's the kind of hard work that returns to you in expansive opportunities, rapid personal growth, and generational wealth creation.

So in 2021, I shared "A simplified timeline of my entrepreneurial emotional roller coaster" in a three-part series on Instagram. It was my documentation of what doing the damn thing actually looks like, since too many people were finding me after I had spent years raising my baselines and thought it was a smooth ride to the top. I wanted to be super clear that I had invested years of hard work, made oodles of mistakes, and pushed through crippling self-doubt to get to the Instagram-worthy highlights.

It was also quite cathartic to go back and look at all my major milestones, since I don't really mark my small wins as much as I could.

Mostly, I wanted to make sure people understood this part that I wrote in the caption:

> *...the interesting thing about *your own* path is even when you wander in what feels like the "wrong direction," years later you look back and realize why you had to go down that path.*

As we take a moment in this chapter to talk about the 40 percent and start to think about moving into action, I want to start by reminding you how meandering this journey can be. So, edited for Insta-level emoji use but otherwise intact, here's a recap of my entrepreneurial path to this moment.

Part I

- It's 2013, and I am acutely aware of how my efforts don't matter as much as the length of time I'm at my company, and I start to question the incentive structure of a typical nine-to-five...
- Resentment around my job grows as I feel more trapped, unappreciated, taken advantage of, and I begin to notice that life is passing me by...

- My beloved dog is unexpectedly killed, which causes a total existential crisis. I can't imagine wasting another day at my current job. After two tear-filled days of blowing off work (they thought I was at a conference), I walk into my boss's office *in my pajamas* and quit my job...lol, not my finest moment but perhaps one of the most important.
- Unexpectedly, he begs me to stay and offers me a hefty raise. I'm left wondering, *If they appreciate my work, why did they treat me the way they did?* I conclude that many employers use fear as a motivator, and I resolve never to subject myself nor anyone who works with me to that kind of treatment. Life is too damn short...
- I start my first business as an event planner. Within one year, it exceeds my previous income and is featured in a few major publications...
- I learn many important lessons, including the following:
  - I love interacting with all kinds of characters.
  - My faith in my ability to figure things out grows exponentially.
  - I'm amazed at how quickly I can build a business—without getting an MBA.
  - I love that my hard work results in earnings that are passed on directly to *me*.
  - I don't give an eff about the color of linens.
  - I feel trapped because events require your physical presence—location independence becomes a top priority.
  - I had started writing on the side and LOVE it.

Part II

- I'm stuck in a city I hate while I wrap up my event planning business. My desire for location independence turns into a nonnegotiable. I decide to focus on copywriting...
- I'm writing for literally anyone. Including an agency that is downright abusive. I am earning 3 cents a word. I'm in debt, crying and drinking a lot...
- I'm accidentally cc'd on an email and find out I am that agency's best writer and they are charging $300+ for pieces I am getting paid $30 to write. I am livid...
- I realize I am a capable writer, but I'm still crippled by self-doubt, imposter syndrome, and fear. I double down on mindset work...
- I take responsibility for where I am in my career (and life) and shift from being a desperate freelancer to a business owner. This isn't some grand overnight transformation; it's made up of small and *consistent* actions that compound over time.
- I suddenly find myself working WAY too much, and my only response to friends and family when they ask how I am is "Busy."
- I go fully freelance and have my first six-figure year as a copywriter, writing for businesses I believe are making a positive impact in the world.
- I realize how doable this is for others. I start telling anyone who will listen (and many who won't, lol) about the freedom in entrepreneurship. I'm basically stopping strangers on the street. I'm so excited.

- I learn how to say NO. No to advice that doesn't sit well with me, no to shitty clients, and no to things that merely "look good" but don't move me closer to my goals. As a result, my work becomes more fun, fulfilling, and successful.
- I lead two people through a path to freelancing I suspect will work—they both quit their jobs within three months. I think, *Holy shit. More people need this.*
- I start to build an online course, which makes me extremely uncomfortable for a number of reasons. (1) I'm terrified it won't actually help people, (2) I have zero desire to plaster my face on things and grow a social media following, and (3) it feels super cliché.
- What keeps me going? Those two people who quit their jobs, and remembering how sad and lost I was when I first started working for myself.

Part III

- Client work is at an all-time high and I'm collecting real results. Having numbers to back up my work feels so. damn. good.
- Cherry on top: I absolutely love my clients.
- After six months of not showering lol, my course is ready for its first launch. It does okay.
- A few months pass and my students are doing well. I'm thrilled (and relieved) they are starting to report real wins!
- I realize what makes my business successful is that I continue to focus on the *value* I deliver.

Logos, fancy websites, Instagram engagement, and other bells and whistles continue not to be my focus.

- I discover one of my clients is not who they say they are. I promptly quit. I'm furious and embarrassed. I seriously consider quitting copywriting altogether.
- I go to Bali to get my head right. Instead, I'm working fifty-plus hours a week—my anxiety skyrockets. I have my first panic attack in over five years.
- Out of desperation, I hire a mentor. At that point in time, she was by far the biggest investment I've ever made in myself—and the best. I begin to get my anxiety under control.
- My anxiety is always a clue. One major realization is that traveling isn't as fulfilling as it once was (I'd been to twenty-three countries in seven years). It feels like I'm collecting experiences rather than building anything substantial.
- I return to Santa Monica, grateful it feels like home. I decide to get back to the basics. My morning routine and community building. I find my flow.
- I host my first student mastermind. I realize my time as an event planner wasn't a total waste after all! It's life-changing for me to meet all these beautiful souls.
- The pandemic hits. I'm terrified for my students. I start hosting weekly work sessions to check in with them.
- My students don't just survive—*they thrive.* Blowing my mind and inspiring me beyond belief.

That was in 2021. Later that year, *Business Insider* featured me in multiple articles helping other people build their own businesses. I spent six weeks in Italy, then South Africa, and I did a live Q&A for my community, standing in a citrus field, surrounded by beehives. This felt like a full-circle moment. Traveling again felt incredible because I'd found balance.

I was also in a relationship with the most incredible man. He was supportive beyond belief; he challenged me, but also held me and reminded me of my strength when things felt uncertain. My students and mentees continued to blow me away with their wins. They were quitting their jobs, helping their partners quit their jobs, generating down payments for their homes, spending more time with their families, and creating opportunities out of thin air.

In 2022, I decided it was time to level up my business. I grew my team from two to twenty-one incredible people, and while initially this was intimidating, it turned out to be one of the most rewarding things I've ever done as an entrepreneur. I love bringing people into our little family and helping them reimagine what their lives can look like. Ben and I got married and pregnant. Life felt so expansive.

In 2023, we moved to Miami and Ben went fully remote. Bennett was born to two parents who are able to be attentive and present with him—an absolute dream come true. Everything I built allowed me to take three months off for maternity leave. My business was ranked #1256 on the Inc. 5000 list, and #24 in education.

Can you see that hidden growth curve in effect?

It's easy to look at where I am today and think, *Wow. Must be nice.* Skipping the montage moments, we forget that it took actual blood, sweat, tears, and a decade's worth of work to get there.

When I was sitting at the table in rehab, growing my free-lance business, I needed it to be small and simple. If I had outright tried to build an eight-figure business with a team to help me while I tried to buy a home and grow my family, all of that darkness would have closed in on me. Hard. I wasn't ready. I needed to identify my values and start the work of getting into alignment first.

Even now, I experience resistance talking about my success. There are still growth edges to find and uncomfortable spaces to explore. But that's why the majority of my time is spent on mindset work—because it's not enough to just see an opportunity and expect to be able to maximize it. You need a foundation in place before you can start building.

The good news is: you've got a pretty good foundation now that you've made it to the end of this book, or at least the raw material to make one. I can't wait to see what's next for you.

Grow to the Moon

A year after writing my timeline on Instagram, I hosted another annual event for my students—it felt amazing to get together with like-minded souls all on the journey to make our lives better. One of the unexpected experiences of the weekend came from a skeleton key I gave to each of them, referencing a poem written by a fourteenth-century poet named Hafez. It goes like this:

The small woman
Builds cages for everyone
She knows.
While the sage,
Who has to duck her head
When the moon is low,

Keeps dropping keys all night long
For the
Beautiful
Rowdy
Prisoners.

This poem was originally sent to me by a student of mine who's become a dear friend. She made it feminine, and I've kept it that way ever since. We intended to spend just a little bit of time on day two of the event listening to people share the "keys" they had picked up so far—maybe twenty minutes tops. An hour and a half later, people shared insight after insight, not just about what they'd learned in the course and at the event, but in the entirety of their lives. It was gorgeous.

They were moved by the imagery of living small, trapped in the cages of fear and scarcity, versus the sage growing until she has to duck because even the moon is in her way. We talked about how we can be both the sage and the prisoner in different areas of our lives, and how remembering this gives us empathy for those who are still prisoners where we've gotten free. We also saw how we can drop keys even when we aren't yet free in every area of our lives. Everyone has wisdom—but it's up to each person to actually use it. It's important to note that while the sage can drop keys; it's up to the prisoners to unlock their own doors. We are all sages, and we are all prisoners.

Even when I'm looking back at my growth and all the cages I've had to unlock, I still see doors I need to open. But whenever I'm focusing on helping others, I can, more easily, stretch into the spaces that make me uncomfortable.

While calling myself a sage makes my self-deprecating heart so uncomfortable, when I'm course-making, recording videos, and posting on social media, I know I'm dropping keys. Even though it pushes up against my fears and limiting beliefs, eventually I can look back and see how much I grew.

I used to be consumed by guilt anytime I'd say no, and now I understand how much better it makes every "yes."

I used to hate the idea of marketing, but I now teach how to make marketing feel aligned.

I used to wait for others to show me what I'm worth, but now I can't unsee my value—or the value of every single person I interact with.

My life's work is to make sure the people around me—as many as possible—have that same realization, no matter what shape that work might take from here.

But it's also not enough to just identify your limiting beliefs and then expect everything to change. If I left you with the knowledge that you can detach your time from money and decide what kind of life you want to build, but without any tangible way to do it, then I'd be leaving you and your brain to the fear party it's dying to throw.

So before we can close out this book and send you on your way toward whatever it is you want to build, we have to revisit the compound effect. We have to identify specific ways you can put that unsexy training montage into the everyday practice of personal *and* business growth, without losing your mind doing it.

The level of freedom, joy, and community I have now didn't show up overnight.

I was suicidal, y'all. I crawled out of that pit of despair one arm over the other, dirt under my fingernails.

And as you already know (but I'll keep telling you anyway), small changes compound into exponential transformation.

Choose Your Own Adventure

One more reminder, louder for those in the back (of the book, ha): literally anything can be turned into a business.

People monetize random shit all day, every day, all over the internet. Think back to the Gen Z'ers unboxing toys and playing video games, or the people doing tarot card readings or using oysters to make cross-shaped pearls on TikTok. Monetization possibilities are limitless, no matter what your niche is. Content creation with ads or sponsors, client work, affiliate marketing, and product sales can all overlap with each other and other types of businesses—meaning you can dig into a revenue stream from almost anywhere. And when the way you make money is untied from your worth or even your identity, it releases pressure and allows you to be more playful in exploring those possibilities.

When I first drafted this chapter, I wanted to lay out all of the possible options you could choose from and then help guide you to a decision.

Instead, I want you to meet Ryan.

Ryan signed up for Write Your Way to Freedom in his early twenties while he had a full-time job as a cook frying chicken. When he made a change, it wasn't because he knew what was on the other side. He just knew something was off and he needed to make a move. I seriously admire that about him—he doesn't let the unknown stop him from taking the next step. If it feels right, he just takes it.

Ryan had stacks of notebooks full of things that he'd written, but he didn't consider himself a writer. When I interviewed him in our community, he told me, "I figured someone would have to do something with [the things I'd written] after I died." But his girlfriend sent him a link to the course, and the pieces came together: writing was already a hobby, and now he could learn how to turn it into a business. So, why not try?

He took the idea that *you make a living from nine to five, but you build an empire from six to ten*, and ran with it. Sprinted, really. Just chipping away at the course every evening after work, he actually finished the material in under a month. He put the foundation for an entire business in place in a matter of weeks. (For the record, that's not typical or even necessary pacing.) But Ryan was ready for change. And for a guy who was trying to find his place in the world, exploring opportunities after work was exactly the shift he needed.

Ryan built experience in his new business by being willing to try new things, well before he felt ready. He says he's a perfectionist and an introvert, but he never waited for perfection and consistently put himself "out there."

His first-choice niche didn't last long—he soon felt like it was misaligned with his values and beliefs and didn't have the energy behind it that he had hoped to find. So he made a change, first to write for therapists and coaches, and then to write for e-commerce. Again, all without worrying about the time he had spent in entirely different spaces. He knew he had been adding to his skill set, learning, and growing all along.

One of the first e-commerce projects he took on was for his girlfriend's mom, who ran a furniture remodeling business on Etsy. He decided to revamp her listings in exchange for data and a testimonial. After reworking all of her product descriptions, she started selling multiple pieces of furniture a week instead of some every few weeks. Those results were enough to give him both faith and credibility to keep building his business—he converted the numbers to percentages, put them in his portfolio with the testimonials she gave him, and leveraged that toward his own confidence and the trust-building he was doing with prospective clients.

The e-commerce niche made it easy to track the analytics of his work and demonstrate value, which made it easier to reach out to new prospective clients with a cold email that offered a specific service with a specific outcome.

Once he could see the tremendous value in the work he did, he knew that his work was actually worth what he charged, which gave him confidence when charging that rate. He explained his process for an initial call with clients, which included offering advice and suggestions without worrying about giving away "too much." Ryan had always wanted to help people, and this was his way to have an impact.

Ryan continued to market his skills by taking podcast interviews and reaching out to brands after he found products he personally loved. He shifted payment structures so that he would get paid in advance and feel more protected while doing the work. He expanded his skills even further, which continued to increase his value until he was taking ten- and twenty-thousand-dollar projects. Regularly.

Now he's ghostwriting books and absolutely killing it.

What started as an evening course, then led to a free project for someone close to him, ultimately changed the course of Ryan's life. And he's still got a lot of life left to enjoy.

When Ryan and I talked again a year and a half later for an updated student success story, he said he was shocked at how much he thought he knew the first time around.

He explained that it wasn't really confidence that drove him in his first months as a business owner. It was the idea that he was going to have to fail a certain amount of times anyway, so why not get it all out of the way up front?

And while he did tell me all about the successes, because those are what stood out, in the follow-up he acknowledged there were bad gigs too. He had clients who didn't see the results they wanted say hurtful things. He had clients disappear and not pay. He had a range of successes and failures because he put himself into a range of experiences.

But he kept going anyway, knowing that failing was just part of the process. This is how he put it: "You have to realize, 'I'm gonna fail a lot. There's gonna be things that go wrong, but I have to keep going—because eventually it's gonna be really good.'"

There are so many unique ways to make money that didn't exist twenty, ten, or even five years ago, and I suspect new ways will continue to emerge. Look at how AI is already shifting the career landscape—in a good way. It's turning out to be an incredible tool and asset to writers, and since the output depends on the input, subject matter experts will always be needed.

Now more than ever before, it's time to think outside the box. To venture off the old-school, prescribed path our parents and grandparents seem stuck on and to go chart a brand-new course.

Speaking of courses, people are told all the time that something like a course creates passive income, but anyone who has gone down that path knows better. It's a fuck-ton of work. Not only the setup but also the maintenance. Things are breaking all the time, content needs to be updated…the only way I can see a bigger digital product like a course being passive is if you hired a team to manage it and fully stepped away. That doesn't mean you shouldn't do a course or sell digital products. My point is that the phrase "passive income" is a shiny, misleading little pot of gold at the end of the online business rainbow.

What we actually want when we think of passive income is the ability to untie your earning potential from your time (in a big way), usually from multiple sources of revenue. Do that, and you'll get the experience of passive income without the illusion that it'll somehow happen like magic.

How do you do that?

By playing.

By experimenting.

By paying attention to what gives you energy and what drains it.

By niching down until you find a space that you love, one adventurous step at a time.

Find a Mentor

I already mentioned that you'll want at least one friend in real life who can support you, and the internet can't be the only place where you get that support. Not forever. And while it's generally a good thing that people are breaking down old-school concepts like needing to have a PhD to teach people about a subject, a consequence of that shift is a growing sea of self-proclaimed experts. You have to be smart about who you engage with and ultimately give your money to.

In freshman year of college, I was shocked to learn that most of the professors in that school hadn't worked in the field that they taught. They were just lifelong teachers. When I transferred schools later on, the professors at my new college were teaching as retirees who had loved their field of work out in the real world. The difference was stark. We didn't just listen to theories—we learned from their actual experience.

So, aside from looking for free, local, or online communities and well-vetted internet courses to boost your support network, it makes a lot of sense to gain real-life experience under the guidance of a mentor. Someone who offers direct guidance around opportunities that lay outside traditional paths.

An opportunity with a good mentor can help you grow your confidence and credibility, often faster than you can in school. When you're working with a mentor, you're in action the whole time. Few mentorships are based on just study or regurgitation. You'll likely walk away from that time with real-life experience that doubles as a portfolio, with case studies or testimonials that lay the foundation for your next right step.

A mentorship is successful when you achieve your goals, not when you finish the material.

So how do you find a mentor?

Start looking!

Social media, Google, and YouTube make it relatively easy to find people who are creating useful content that gets you closer to where you want to be. And because people are obsessed with likes and followers, the creation of free content is at an all-time high. Put those obnoxious algorithms to work in your favor—the more you engage with content you like, the more Facebook and Instagram are going to recommend similar people and paths. Eventually, you'll find someone worth reaching out to.

I leaned on this strategy in Bali, when I started feeling lonely every day around 3:00 p.m., thinking about how everyone I loved was asleep on the other side of the world. Instead of hitting rock bottom, I started journaling. Specifically, about how I wanted to find a mentor. Not long after, a woman came across my newsfeed who lived in Bali and worked with—get this—*sober entrepreneurial women who struggled with anxiety.*

I immediately signed up for her emails. As they started coming in, day by day, I was blown away by how they were speaking directly to me and my struggles. It was like she was in my head. I reached out to her to start a mentorship program—by far the biggest investment I'd made in myself and my business up to that point.

She challenged me to reexamine my stories around sensations in my body that I had been quickly labeling as anxiety. I remember explaining how I used to wake up with anxiety, thinking I was just generally an anxious person. She reminded me that your body releases hormones, and the neurotransmitters that wake you from your sleep are the very ones that cause sensations of anxiety-like adrenaline.

I was also terrified to drive a moped while I was there (something that's essential if you want to be able to get around), and again, she invited me to be really curious about the sensations I was labeling as fear and anxiety. Upon further examination, I realized those feelings were similar to excitement and arousal. My heart was racing, my attention was focused, and my belly was warm. I could think of those feelings as *excited*, not anxious. This thought process truly changed my life and had me questioning "truths" I had about myself, which ultimately released a lot of limiting beliefs, and I could only do it because of her specific expertise and our mentorship relationship.

When you're looking for a mentor, remember that they aren't always advertising for mentees. It can happen a little more organically than that—which means you have to ask the people you want to learn from.

If there's someone you admire, someone who has achieved a goal that you've set for yourself, then start up a conversation: "Have you ever considered having a mentorship program or taking on a mentee? I would love to learn from you."

Be sure to offer your help so it's a benefit to them too. Mentoring someone is very energy- and time-expensive, although rewarding. You have something to offer them too, even if it's enthusiasm for what they do and taking a few time-consuming tasks off their plate. Put yourself out there. It's going to be the beautiful beginning of a relationship. I can feel it.

Reminders, Hacks, and Tools to Get You Going

This book hasn't been a full-on how-to guide, mostly because the "how" changes so rapidly in the digital world that there's no way to stay relevant for long. But there are certain hacks that you can use in almost any business that will make a difference right away.

This is a list of the most impactful behaviors I've implemented in my life.

Declare your intentions (and keep an eye out for opportunity). Try this exercise, simply saying an intention out loud with your hand on your heart. Yes, I mean right now.

Maybe it's one of the following:

- "I'm open to the possibility of a career that gives me more freedom and purpose."
- "I'm open to the idea that life can be easier than I've let it be so far."
- "I'm a forever student and open to new ways of earning money and living life."
- "I would love to know what my next right step is."
- "I am open to earning money in new and unexpected ways."

If you want signs and opportunities to start showing up, then you've got to start showing the universe you're ready and willing to do the work. Put yourself into situations where the opportunities you're looking for might be found. Entrepreneurial events, YouTube rabbit holes, online communities—all of it counts. Tell safe people what you're working on and thinking about. Permit yourself to share without having it all figured out. Get out into the world with clear intentions, then see what you'll find and what might find you.

Prioritize prime time for growth. The best hour of your day needs to be spent on you. Period. Whether that's first thing in the morning or at 2:00 a.m. Don't open your email. Don't jump into client work. Ideally, don't focus on anything but yourself during this time. Even if you have to wake up a bit earlier (yes, I know having kids makes that harder).

How you prioritize your growth may be different day by day or change through the seasons of your life, but the most important thing is that you are attempting to consistently spend the best hour of your day on yourself. When you're growing as a human, you're growing as an entrepreneur, and vice versa. It's a reinforcing cycle. Challenge your self-limiting beliefs, improve your emotional reactivity, and reflect on what's working and what isn't. Protect space for your creative practices or to get into a state of flow. Get quiet, and check in with your intuition and the universe. Leave space to receive clues about your next right steps. After taking this step seriously for a little while, you'll start to believe me when I say that you deserve your best.

For real, though, *prioritize your time.* I haven't always been perfect about my intention to have shorter workdays. There are phases where I catch myself working ten-hour days again, feeling miserable and burned out. But I see it and correct it now. I push all of my meetings back to 10:00 a.m. start times,

I make space to work out, I set a stop time, and make sure I walk away by then. I try to feel human again, instead of pushing myself to be a machine. That's what I want for you too.

Batch your work. As an entrepreneur, your calendar is your own. Maximize it. Put the most important tasks first—I like to have at least one important thing that I plan to get done first. If I don't have time for anything else at the end of the day, those less-important tasks just move over to the next. Keep in mind, the important task might be the scary task. The thing you're procrastinating on most. If I notice I've moved something over days in a row, then it takes the number one spot on the calendar. This helps me stop myself from checking all the tiny tasks off first, which is tempting because it looks like I've moved through most of my to-do list.

If you're struggling with procrastination, try the Pomodoro Technique. That's basically setting a timer for just twenty or thirty minutes to tackle something challenging or scary, instead of thinking it has to take up the whole afternoon and imagining how awful that's going to be. Procrastination usually has an emotional motivator (often a fear), and you can hijack it by proving to yourself the task isn't so big and bad after all. And even if it's still terrifying after you get started, you'll have made twenty more minutes' progress than you might have otherwise.

Focus on value. Stop. charging. by. the. hour. If you're just starting your entrepreneurial journey and don't know what to do next, I recommend learning a high-value skill set that creates some kind of transformation for another person so you can qualify or quantify that change and charge for it.

Let's be clear, though. Marketing is an example of a more tangible value, while things like art have a more subjective or perceived value—but one is not *inherently* more valuable than the other. Perceived value is impactful and powerful because of the effect it has on a person. Subjective value isn't less value—it just means you have to get in front of the right person or get clear about what the effect is going to be.

Plan in ninety-day increments. Set big goals, but don't worry about every single step from here to there. Just focus on the next ninety days and the baby steps you can actually take in that time. Leave the rest to Future You. Future You is going to be more prepared for future decisions anyway. Chances are, your plan will change, so planning too far ahead isn't in your best interest. This practice changed my life. I'm less anxious. I'm more focused on what I can control. I'm able to realign my choices every few months, checking in with what's energizing or draining me and how I can plan to do more of one and less of the other.

As soon as goals are on the table, people start jumping to future problems, like *What if I get too many clients?* If it's not a problem for you right now, it's not a problem that needs a plan. Want to have your first $8,000 month as a freelancer? Spend an hour a day focusing on client acquisition and an hour growing your skill set and getting feedback. That's all.

It's honestly incredible what you can accomplish in three months. And if you can't trust Future You to solve problems outside of that window, then you probably can't trust Present You, either. In that case, I suggest putting self-trust work on your next ninety-day plan. Make small promises to yourself, then keep them. "Today, I'll work on my project for thirty minutes." Then do it. Again and again. When you don't get to it one day, don't beat yourself up, simply course correct and get back on track. Remember that even working on not beating yourself up is part of the process. You're a rocket on the way to the moon, my friend.

Wait for the growth curve. Exponential growth happens when you commit to the small stuff. Like Ryan, my timeline has a sharp growth curve to it, and most of my students experience the same thing.

At the beginning of that curve, you don't see the results that are building. You're creating invisible momentum. You have to operate on faith that if you keep showing up, it'll happen—much faster than waiting for minuscule annual raises and eventually retirement plans to trickle in.

Maybe the first few months will bounce around a couple hundred bucks, but consistency and personal growth always pay off. It seems like you go from that trickle of income to a sudden rush, and before you know it, your new normal is $10,000 a month and you're not even sure what happened. Remember Cassidy?

Take back your attention. Companies are profiting off of your attention. At this point, it's a currency all on its own. So I give you full permission to hoard every last drop of it.

Your attention is precious. And most people are allowing things like emails, social media, the news, and notifications to hijack it throughout the day. Carefully feed your mind just like you would your body. Yes, it's good to know what's going on in the world, but only to a point. As soon as your attention is diverted away from becoming a better human, it's time to take a step back.

Stick it to the media. Turn off all the notifications on your phone, don't allow TV to run in the background, and even switch your phone to silent or airplane mode from time to time. Shut down anything that keeps you from "spending" your attention in places where you can actually get some value in return. Take back your attention, and you take control of your life.

Outsource and delegate. And when you do outsource, *empower the people you hire*. Be the kind of person people want to work for. Pay on time. Set clear expectations. Let them know you appreciate them often. Create a space where people can grow. Don't use fear as a motivator. Empower people.

I don't subscribe to the patriarchal bullshit that uses fear as a motivator, and I don't think you should outsource work for the lowest possible price you can pay someone. Outsourcing as an individual entrepreneur was made famous by Tim Ferriss in his book *The 4-Hour Work Week*. He talks about how the ability to outsource tasks to other countries where you can pay people less is no longer only accessible to massive corporations but now to individuals—all you need is a laptop to access a website like Fiverr, where you can hire people from the Philippines to do digital work for a fraction of the price of hiring an American.

I've got to be honest. When I started reading that section of the book, I was disgusted. I even put it down. My mind immediately went to outsourcing as a way to take advantage of other people. But as I checked my mindset around this, I realized it's up to me to decide what I pay the people who work for me. I don't have to take advantage of those I employ. I know that the ability to hire across borders has helped many entrepreneurs get incredible businesses off the ground, and hopefully without taking advantage of anyone. And to take it a step further, this is getting money into the hands of people who pre-internet times didn't have access to something as well paying. Benefiting people in other countries while giving power to small businesses is kind of sticking it to large corporations. Win.

When I started hiring people, I didn't have a good model for how to treat them. Everywhere I had worked up until that point had treated me as if they owned me, and I should be eternally grateful to be there. All I knew was that I wanted better for anyone who worked for me. So it took some trial and error, as well as challenging some old-school beliefs around work relationships, but now working with my team and getting to pay people well for the work they do is one of my favorite parts of my job.

Refining is just as important as scaling. When you check in with yourself and find that something makes you feel drained, stop doing that thing. Or at least make a plan to stop. As soon as you get smarter about your energy and become more efficient with your time, it feels like scaling, whether or not you've actually grown your business.

Even though you aren't charging per hour, keep an eye on what you're making relative to how much time you're spending. I think of it as a secret hourly rate: know what you're actually earning and use that rate as a measurement of growth. Can you increase it by focusing on higher-level tasks while delegating lower-level tasks? Can you add something to your business that increases value and allows you to charge more? You don't have to think about scaling (unless you want to), but you absolutely should evaluate and reevaluate every aspect of your business all along the way, with an eye toward making it work better for you and your people.

Find your people. It's crucial that you surround yourself with people who are on a journey similar to yours, especially because you're likely to be the first of your family and friends to venture into entrepreneurship. If you don't actively seek out those who have the same destination as you, you're going to be limited by your environment.

But you don't *have* to move across the country like I did to surround yourself with entrepreneurs. There are powerful online communities that have allowed us to connect around our interests and desires without being limited to where we live. No matter what you're interested in doing, there is already a community out there waiting for you with open arms. Seek them out.

Beware of well-meaning but uninformed advice. Keep an eye out for advice that's rooted in fear, or that comes from someone who's living a completely different life than the one you're building.

Here are two questions to ask when someone's giving you advice: Has this person been where you're trying to go? Does this person embody something you'd like for yourself? If you can't get at least one solid yes, then the advice isn't meant for you.

Last but not least: not everything is a mindset issue.

We're done with mindset gaslighting.

Yes, working with literally hundreds of people at a time, I can say that mindset issues are the most common underlying issue. *And* they aren't our only obstacles. There are seriously real limitations in people's lives that can't be discounted as mindset. Some career choices and business-building paths are going to be extra challenging no matter how much you manifest them and believe in abundance.

Be gracious with yourself and honest about the limitations that you're up against. And be so, so careful with others, especially if you start creating content or teaching people in any way. It's a hard balance to strike because a lot of times, people do have mindset blocks that keep them from accessing what you're teaching to the extent you know is possible. But the human experience is nuanced. Not everything fits into a box.

Limitations are real. Trauma is real. Discrimination is real. Racism is real. Addiction is real.

You don't know what's going on for the people you interact with, and writing off their experience as a mindset issue 100 percent of the time holds everyone back.

If you're the one experiencing resistance, it's up to you to examine whether or not your strong emotional reaction is potential self-sabotage out of fear of the unknown, *or* if it's your authentic self trying to get your attention to tell you that the thing is not for you.

Only you can cultivate self-awareness, strengthen your personal trust, and move toward a more authentic you who can decide what's aligned and what isn't. And if you're anything like me, that work will include unpacking a lot of conditioning and releasing a lot of "shoulds" around what your life is supposed to look like.

The Best Bet

I talk about emotion, mindset, and intuition because they're key to a strong entrepreneur. These aspects are often associated with femininity and are even more often considered weak or capricious. But what I've come to realize is they are a strength. That's a huge part of my message, and it speaks to a lot of people starting out as entrepreneurs. We're not one type of person. We're not building one kind of business. We need more nuanced conversations.

What you decide to do in your career today probably won't be what you're doing five or ten years from now, and that's more than okay. Our brains love novelty; it's what keeps us resilient and strong. Each time we push past imposter syndrome or a new set of fears or self-doubt, we gain more faith in our abilities to figure things out and more strength for the next time those challenges arise.

Venturing out to create a career that's perfect for you means you're going to meander down paths that are not quite right. The beautiful part is that this journey will shape-shift with you as you grow and change, and the not-quite-right paths become a stepping stone toward the next one.

This is also why it's essential for people to teach and mentor others once we have discovered new ways of earning money and building a life in alignment with our values. We need more paths to entrepreneurship. More people highlighting paths they've paved or discovered. More people speaking from their own experience, in their own way.

And yes, that includes you.

Every day, I work with students who were once where I was when I started my business, and sometimes I still forget how it feels to be at the beginning.

Every week, I answer questions about crippling fear, self-doubt, and imposter syndrome—and sometimes I still forget how intense that can be.

To tap back into what it feels like to be a newbie, I have this image of myself I think of just before I hop onto the weekly live Q&A in my community. It's Past Sarah in her tiny, dark apartment, crippled by fear, depression, and anxiety. There are too many empty red-wine bottles falling out of the recycling, and she's crying a lot. But she's showing up each day and trying to get better because somewhere deep down, she has a glimmer of hope for a better future.

Writing this book was an exercise in remembering Past Sarah, too. It has been a way to face the fear and remember how strong and daunting it can be. Not just in recalling the stories, but because it put me back in the shoes of a newbie. I had to learn and grow through this process just like I did with the others. And it was worth every second.

I wrote this book for you so you could connect with your own entrepreneurial future, and along the way, it reconnected me with my past and what it took to get here.

Each time we share our stories, we shine a light on new possibilities for others and bring new perspective to our own self-belief. You'll be amazed at how fast and exponentially you'll grow. Things that were once daunting will become your new habits, and when you look back, you'll see a different version of yourself—a younger you that you're so, so proud of.

You have an incredible abundance of opportunity and resources to make the changes that add up to a rich, beautiful, and fulfilling experience during your time on this planet, and I want nothing more than for you to wake up every day with a smile on your face because you're excited for what's to come.

When you decide to be a dream seeker and a forever student, your life begins to change immediately. You're opening yourself up to an entire world of new possibilities. It won't always be easy, but it will be the right kind of hard. The rewarding kind.

You have this precious, free life that you truly get to create. You can make it look precisely how *you* want it to look, and you can get there as fast or slow as you want.

You're amazing, my friend.

I'd bet on you every time.

Care to join me?

THE WORLD AS I SEE IT

I want more people—*good people*—to be entrepreneurs.

I want more people to see the dick-rocket-making, Lambo-posing, black-T-shirt entrepreneurs as the exception, not the rule. Fuck those guys. They're not evidence that the world's a disaster. *We're* evidence that the world is full of kind-hearted, empathetic people doing our best.

They don't set our standards. We do. And we have so many cooler things to do than to worry about whether we've hit our bro-quotient for the quarter.

And I know it's going to be hard. We have to make different choices, and sometimes those choices can feel impossible.

But I promise you, even the smallest daily choices add up. They're why I'm the millionaire instead of the drunk right now—because Past Sarah decided that Future Sarah was worth more than I'd given her. And even if I couldn't see how small changes would add up or when the payoff would come, I had just enough faith to try.

It isn't easy. Good choices are hard to make from a bad place. Momentum isn't on your side yet, so you have to work that much harder to get things moving. But this isn't Sisyphus's story—the Greek king who was doomed by the gods to repeatedly push a boulder up a hill for eternity. This is *your* story, and momentum will catch up to you eventually. You might not even see it coming, but one day you'll look back and realize you've become another version of yourself who's living out dreams you didn't even know you could have.

The only difference between those versions of me is the choices that I started to make and still make today. Nothing more, nothing less.

No magic happened. No one saved me. I'm capable of being both of these versions, even today. I know it's only my choices keeping me from rock bottom, and *I can always stay above rock bottom.*

Now that I have some momentum on my side, course corrections come faster and easier, and rock bottom looks further and further away. But momentum doesn't always mean ease.

It also doesn't mean every choice I make is right or has to be right or even *can* be right.

I've woken up in a panic a few times since Bali.

I've worked too many hours, too many times.

I've wondered what I got myself into and how I could ever get out again.

Misalignment still hurts. It's still uncomfortable. But I know what it is now. I can see what's off much more quickly, and I have so much more trust in my ability to make those adjustments and bring it back in line again.

The more you raise your baselines, the higher you're starting from when it's time to course correct. And change is *always* going to be necessary. Your choices are always going to matter. You're building a whole life here, and that's a dynamic, shifting thing. This isn't about happily ever after any more than it's about escaping to the woods.

This is about you unlocking your cages.

It's about picking up keys from everyone who's gone before you and dropping them for anyone who's coming behind.

It's about all of us,

Beautiful

Rowdy

Prisoners

growing together until we're ducking under the moon.

Everything builds on itself.

Everything is helping you grow.

You are being pointed in the right direction. You've just gotta take the next baby step.

ACKNOWLEDGMENTS

To my husband, Ben. Your love is the most healing thing I've ever experienced in this life. You've taught me to be braver than I knew was possible. Your ability to grow and level up is unmatched. I'm beyond grateful for you.

To my dear friend, Emily. You've championed me through the darkest seasons of my life and helped me love parts of myself I thought were unlovable. You're a gift to this world and I'm so grateful to call you my best friend.

And to my sweet baby boy, Bennett. You've expanded my heart and given everything I do more meaning. You show me the world through fresh, wonder-filled eyes. May you grow up with a thirst for knowledge and a heart full of kindness.

ABOUT THE AUTHOR

Sarah Turner is an eight-figure business owner, entrepreneur, and mentor on a mission to demystify what it means to build your own online business in today's world. She specializes in combining mindset work with entrepreneurial skills to create successful business strategies. Her copy is responsible for tens of millions of dollars in sales.

Sarah has over half a million people in her global online community and has helped over six thousand of her students using her programs Write Your Way to Freedom and Let's Build Your Online Business to supplement, replace, or exceed their income. You can find her on Instagram and YouTube, or join her email list at officialsarahturner.com.

Milton Keynes UK
Ingram Content Group UK Ltd.
UKHW050437160424
441219UK00010B/84/J